W9-BIH-839

COOL CAREERS WITHOUT COLLEGE FOR

NATURE

LOVERS

COOL CAREERS WITHOUT COLLEGE FOR
NATURE
LOVERS

**KATIE
HAEGELE**

ROSEN
PUBLISHING®

New York

Published in 2002, 2009 by The Rosen Publishing Group, Inc.
29 East 21st Street, New York, NY 10010

Copyright © 2002, 2009 by The Rosen Publishing Group, Inc.

Revised Edition

All rights reserved. No part of this book may be reproduced in any form without permission in writing from the publisher, except by a reviewer.

Library of Congress Cataloging-in-Publication Data

Haegele, Katie.
Cool careers without college for nature lovers / Katie Haegele.
p. cm. — (Cool careers without college)
Includes bibliographical references (p.).
Summary: Profiles the characteristics of and qualifications needed for twelve jobs that involve working with nature.
ISBN-13: 978-1-4358-5245-7 (lib. binding)
1. Natural history—Vocational guidance—Juvenile literature.
[1. Natural history—Vocational guidance. 2. Vocational guidance.]
I. Title. II. Series.
QH49 .H34 2001
508'.023—dc21

2001003911

Manufactured in the United States of America

CONTENTS

	Introduction	7
1	Christmas Tree Farmer	9
2	Commercial Fisher	20
3	Ranch Hand	31
4	Ecotourism Planner	40
5	Groundskeeper	52
6	Teacher/Naturalist	63
7	Park Ranger	74
8	Urban Gardener	84
9	Whale Watcher	96
10	River Guide	106
11	Wildland Fire Manager	117
12	Nature Photographer	127
	Glossary	138
	Index	141

INTRODUCTION

When you hear the word "career," do you think of large, monolithic corporations, featureless glass office buildings, and sterile, claustrophobic office cubicles? Do you imagine hours of photocopying, shuffling papers, and staring bleary-eyed at a computer monitor under bleak florescent lights? What if you were offered the opportunity to work on a ship that sailed the sea in search of great big whales or voyaged to remote, unspoiled areas of the world, such as the Arctic Circle? What if you could be living and working in a national park, leading a cattle drive on horseback, or transforming an abandoned city lot into a beautiful green space?

For some lucky people, work means being outside every day, interacting closely with the environment, and pursuing a passion for nature. Many cool careers exist for nature lovers, and many of them do not require a college degree in order to get your foot in the door. In this book, you will be introduced to many jobs that will allow you to earn money in the great outdoors. All of these jobs emphasize hands-on experience as much as formal academic training. So if you have a passion for the work and are willing to initially perform "grunt" duties for low pay, you should find opportunities for advancement before long. If advancement is dependent upon academic training, many of these jobs provide the necessary courses and programs. In addition, courses taken at a community college or technical school can also often satisfy job requirements.

Deriving a sense of satisfaction and fulfillment from a job is often a question of pursuing your interests. If you wish to spend every workday in nature, do not assume that such a desire is an idle daydream. You can make a living from your passion for the outdoors, and this book will show you how to go about finding a job that benefits both you and the environment.

1

CHRISTMAS TREE FARMER

Christmas may come only once a year, but Christmas tree farmers are busy on every one of the 364 other days, too! In fact, it is during the summer that tree farmers work the most and earn the most money. If you can combine a knack for cultivating trees with good communication skills and some business sense, you could build your own business—and a very lucrative career.

A farmer tends to Christmas trees on her tree farm in Texas.

Description

The initial investment needed to start a tree farm can be large because it takes from six to twelve years for the first crop to grow to selling size. One of the reasons Christmas tree farming can be profitable, however, is that fir and pine trees can flourish on marginal or less fertile land. This type of land is far less expensive to purchase.

Christmas tree farmers need to be knowledgeable about trees in general and popular Christmas tree species in particular. One crop of trees requires a year's work, and the yield is not always high. In 2002, the top 5 percent of the farms (farms of 100 acres or more) sold 61 percent of their trees, and the top 26 percent (farms of 20 acres or more) sold 84 percent of their trees. Nearly 22,000 American farms were producing conifers for the cut Christmas tree market that year, and 446,996 acres were planted in Christmas trees.

A typical Christmas tree farm's cycle begins in March and April, when farmers plant a crop of new trees with seedlings that are grown from seed in beds or greenhouses. A seedling is a small tree that is usually between eight and sixteen inches tall. The planting is done either by hand or with the help of a planting machine that is mounted on a tractor.

In the spring and summer, farmers must pay close attention to the upkeep of the grounds where their trees grow. Weeds and overgrown grass, which compete with the trees for space and water, can damage the undersides of the trees, making them less attractive and harder to sell. Fire prevention is another reason for being diligent about keeping grass and weeds cut down. The grass between the trees must be mowed and the weeds controlled by covering them with mulch. An absence of grass and weeds will also keep away mice, which often kill trees by eating their bark. Insects and disease can also become a problem at this time of the year. Pruning, or the removal of infested or diseased

A customer buys a Christmas tree from a tree lot in Jacksonville, Florida.

trees, can help control the problem and prevent it from spreading to other trees in the crop.

During the summer months, the young trees are shaped through pruning. The cone shape and dense foliage growth that customers look for when choosing a tree is not natural. Pruning prevents the trees from growing too tall and also encourages them to branch more quickly, creating a full, bushy appearance.

Fall represents the busiest time of year for Christmas tree farmers. By October, the trees can be harvested and shipped. Some farmers allow families to choose and cut their own trees. Other farmers harvest the trees themselves and gather the cut trees together, selling them in an open area near the farm's entrance. Still others harvest the trees and ship them to city vendors. Before a tree is shipped, it must be shaken out and baled using a machine that presses the tree's branches together against the trunk, holding them in place with twine or plastic netting. This protects the tree from damage to its branches and makes it easier to handle when loading and unloading. In addition, some farmers dig up smaller trees and place them in pots, selling them to families who want a living tree that they can plant in their yard after Christmas. However the farmers choose to harvest and sell them, the trees must be ready for the early-bird buyers by the day after Thanksgiving.

Tree farmers can take some time off for the holidays, but right after Christmas, their work begins again. February and March are when the trees are culled, which means the "Charlie Brown" trees that will not be easy to sell are removed. The winter months are also devoted to equipment repair and property maintenance.

Education/Training

You do not need to get a special degree to learn how to cultivate and sell Christmas trees. Business skills are essential but can be learned through experience. According to the

Fun Facts

From the National Christmas Tree Association

- There are approximately 35 million real Christmas trees sold in North America every year.
- An estimated 175,000 real Christmas trees are sold via the Internet or catalog and shipped. For every real Christmas tree harvested, up to three seedlings are planted in its place the following spring.
- There are about one million acres in production for growing Christmas trees. Each acre provides the daily oxygen requirements for eighteen people. Trees also act as natural air filters, removing up to thirteen tons of airborne pollutants per acre per year.
- There are about 15,000 Christmas tree growers in North America, and over 100,000 people are employed full- or part-time in the industry. Christmas trees are grown in all fifty states.
- Christmas trees are grown in all fifty states, but the top Christmas tree producing states are Oregon, North Carolina, Michigan, Pennsylvania, Wisconsin, and Washington.
- The top selling Christmas trees are balsam fir, Douglas fir, Fraser fir, Scotch pine, Virginia pine, and white pine.

> - It can take as long as fifteen years to grow a tree of suitable height for selling (about six feet), but the average growing time is seven years.

New Hampshire Christmas Tree Promotion Board, many tree farms in New Hampshire have their own education programs. Working at a nursery or farm will give you some background. Your best bet is to contact one of the state chapters of the National Christmas Tree Association to request more information and find out about joining. The NCTA will help you get in touch with a farmer who can answer your questions.

Profile

Bruce Niedermeier, Christmas tree farmer
Grew up in Milwaukee, Wisconsin
Eagle Boy Scout
Active in 4-H
Worked in a corporate job for four years and then bought a tree farm from his father, who had begun tree farming as a postretirement project.

WHAT'S A NORMAL DAY LIKE FOR YOU?
This is a really great job! I left the corporate world to do this. It's especially fun because it has an annual cycle.

There's so much to do, but I have winters off. Plus, part of my farm is dedicated to "choose and cut"—this is the really good part. I get to meet every customer. Often, we end up having great conversations, and I meet interesting people whom I never would have otherwise encountered.

HOW DO CHRISTMAS TREES GET SO PERFECT LOOKING?

We shape the trees with knives. Normally, most trees grow a lot on the top and bottom, and the sides have no growth. We bring the top down to a set height, and this determines how dense or loose the tree is. From here, we use knives to shape the trees like cones. Consumers like perfect trees.

ANY ADVICE FOR PEOPLE WHO WANT TO OPEN A CHRISTMAS TREE FARM?

I think people have to get in touch with themselves to know what makes them happy, even if it's not what friends and family say. Tree growers are the nicest people I've ever worked with, so very nice and giving.

FOR MORE INFORMATION

ASSOCIATIONS

Balsam Fir Christmas Tree Growers of Canada
http://www.evergreenbalsam.ns.ca

Canadian Christmas Tree Growers
http://www.christmastree.net/home_eng.htm

Christmas Tree Farm Network
http://www.christmas-tree.com

National Christmas Tree Association
http://www.christmastree.org

North Carolina Christmas Tree Association
http://www.ncchristmastrees.com

Pennsylvania Christmas Tree Growers Association
http://www.christmastrees.org

WEB SITES

California Christmas Tree Association Research Library
http://www.cachristmas.com/research.htm

Christmas Tree Farms
http://www.ag.auburn.edu/hort/landscape/christmastreehistory.html
An interesting article about the tradition of Christmas tree growing.

Christmas Tree Production Overview
http://hammock.iafs.ufl.edu

Economics of Growing an Acre of White Pines
http://www.ext.vt.edu/pubs/forestry/420-081/420-081.html

50 Careers in Trees
http://www.urbanforest.org/treecareers

Growing Christmas Trees in Illinois
http://www.ag.uiuc.edu/~vista/html_pubs/xmas/xmas.html
Extensive information packet, available free online.

Growing Christmas Trees in Newfoundland and Labrador
http://www.nr.gov.nl.ca/agric/crops/xmas_trees.stm
Information on the business of tree farming, provided by the
    Canadian government.

Species for Christmas Tree Planting in Virginia
http://www.ext.vt.edu/pubs/forestry/420-082/420-082.html

BOOKS

Buffi, Mike. *The Gardener's Guide to Planting and Growing Trees.*
    London, England: Lorenz Books, 2007.

Hicks, Ivan. *Tricks with Trees: Growing, Manipulating and Pruning.*
    London, England: Pavilion, 2007.

Watson, Bob. *Trees: Their Use, Management, Cultivation and Biology: A
    Comprehensive Guide.* Ramsbury, England: Crowood Press, 2006.

MAGAZINES

Christmas Trees
http://www.christmastreesmagazine.com

MULTIMEDIA

Christmas Tree Farm Network
http://www.christmas-tree.com
Includes an online directory of retail and wholesale Christmas tree
    farms in the United States.

Morrill Digital Library: Christmas Trees
http://web.aces.uiuc.edu/aim/ExtensionArticles/
    extart.forestry.christree.htm
Download a video on shearing and culturing Christmas trees.

**Virginia Cooperative Extension, Insect Pests of Christmas Trees
    Slide Show**
http://www.ext.vt.edu/departments/entomology/christmas

2

COMMERCIAL FISHER

Working as a commercial fisher is not always easy. The work can be physically demanding, and it often takes place in remote locations and harsh weather conditions. This job choice has some definite perks, however, such as a very independent life spent on the open sea in some of the most beautiful and unspoiled places in the world.

Description

Commercial fishers need to go where the fish are. Seasonal as well as year-round jobs are available in parts of Washington, Alaska, Florida, New England, Canada, Mexico, and Ireland—wherever there is port access to freshwater or saltwater fish and it is permissible to catch and sell seafood.

Commercial fishers catch fish and other marine life (such as lobsters and shrimp) for use as food, bait, or animal feed. They often fish hundreds of miles from shore in large boats that can hold tens of thousands of pounds of fish. Time away from their home port can last for several weeks or even months. Work on the ship is a cycle of strenuous activity followed by quiet lulls. Netting and hauling the fish in are exhausting activities that require great physical strength and endurance, but a period of rest is enjoyed when the ship sails to its home port or another fishing ground.

Most commercial fishing vessels are staffed by a crew that includes a captain, a first mate, a boatswain, and deckhands. A captain plans and supervises the entire fishing expedition. He or she draws up a budget and decides what fish will be pursued, where the crew will fish, how the fish will be caught, how long the trip will last, and how the catch will be sold upon return to port. The captain will also make sure the boat is in proper working order, buy the necessary supplies and equipment, monitor all weather information, and chart the ship's course using compasses, charts, and tables. A captain must have a thorough knowledge of navigation, boat handling skills, weather patterns, radio-telephone techniques, and the use of electronic gear. He or she must also be able to make good decisions quickly and calmly in emergencies, train and manage a crew with skill and tact, and ensure that fish are handled properly so that they can be safely eaten by consumers. Almost all captains are self-employed, and many own at least some share of their ship.

The first mate serves as the captain's assistant and operates the ship and directs the crew when the captain is off duty. The first mate also organizes and directs the actual fishing activity and sailing operations, such as gathering, preserving, storing, and unloading the catch and maintaining and repairing the ship. He or she must be able to perform all of the captain's duties as well as those of the deckhands should an emergency make his or her assistance necessary.

A boatswain acts as a supervisor of the deckhands, directing them in the performance of the ship's sailing and fishing operations. The boatswain also repairs fishing gear, equipment, and nets, if necessary. The deckhands

A fisherman hauls a load of shrimp out of the waters of Ipswich Bay, Massachusetts.

are responsible for loading and unloading supplies and equipment; untying the lines that moor a ship to the dock; letting out and hauling in the nets; cleaning, preserving, and storing the catch; unloading the catch upon return; and keeping the decks clear and clean and the ship's engines and equipment running smoothly. Deckhands must be in good health, extremely coordinated and mechanically inclined, and very strong. Most commercial fishers begin their careers as deckhands.

Fishermen use large nets spread between the main ship and a smaller boat to catch fish.

Education/Training

The most common way to get a job on a fishing boat is to "walk the docks" at the fishing ports, going from boat to boat asking captains for a job. No formal academic requirements exist, though some high schools offer two-year vocational-technical programs in commercial fishing. Many fishers learn the trade from family members already working in the industry. Operators of large commercial fishing boats must complete a Coast Guard–approved training course. In addition,

Did You Know . . . ?

- Commercial fishing has one of the highest proportions of self-employed workers in the North American workforce.
- Almost all captains eventually become self-employed, and most of them will own (fully or in part) one or more fishing ships.
- A commercial fishing trip may require being at sea for several weeks or even months, often hundreds of miles from home port.
- Fishing boats are much more comfortable today than they used to be. Many modern-day boats include televisions and shower stalls.
- Roughly one out of ten commercial fishers is female.

some community colleges and universities offer courses in seamanship, boat operations, marine safety, navigation, boat repair and maintenance, and first aid.

Following are some training programs and vocational schools where you can begin to learn the ropes of commercial fishing:

Alaska Vocational Technical Center offers an extensive selection of classes in marine and fisheries skills. Contact AVTEC Admissions Office, P.O. Box 889, Seward, AK 99664, or call them at (907) 224-3322.

Educational Training Co., in Sitka, Alaska, offers five-day advanced survival training courses as well as land and sea survival courses for individuals, companies, communities, and schools. Contact Dug or Susan Jensen at (907) 747-3008, or e-mail survival@ptialaska.net.

Outlook

According to the U.S. Department of Labor, fishers and fishing vessel operators held about 38,000 jobs in 2006. About two out of three were self-employed. Most fishing takes place off the coasts, and the most coastal fishing takes place in Alaska, the Gulf Coast, Virginia, California, and New England. The highest total volume of fish are caught in Alaska, according to the National Marine Fisheries Service. Many fishers are seasonal workers and positions are usually filled by people who work primarily in other occupations, such as teachers, or by students. The industry is getting smaller, mainly because pollution and excessive fishing in the past have depleted fish stocks. Job prospects for commercial fishers have been on the decline, but the U.S.

Department of Labor expects that sportfishing boats will continue to provide some job opportunities.

FOR MORE INFORMATION

ASSOCIATIONS

Atlantic Salmon Federation
http://www.asf.ca

Canadian Department of Fisheries and Oceans (DFO)
http://www.dfo-mpo.gc.ca

Caribbean Fisheries Management Council—NOAA
http://www.caribbeanfmc.com

Marine Stewardship Council
http://www.msc.org

New England Fishery Management Council
http://www.nefmc.org

South Atlantic Fishery Management Council
http://www.safmc.nmfs.gov

JOB BANKS

Alaska Fishing Jobs Clearinghouse
http://www.fishingjobs.com

Fishjobs: The Seafood Industry Jobs Network
http://www.fishjobs.com

Maritime Jobs: Maritime Employment Referral Company
http://www.maritimejobs.com

WEB SITES

Commercial Fishing News
http://www.onlinemariner.com

Fishing Works: All Things Fishing
http://www.FishingWorks.com

The Fish Sniffer Online
http://www.imhooked.com

National Fisherman Online
http://www.nationalfisherman.com

Sea Fishing
http://www.worldseafishing.com

U.S. Department of Labor: Fishers and Fishing Vessel Operators
http://stats.bls.gov/OCO/OCOS177.HTM

BOOKS

Bowstern, Moe. *Xtra Tuf!* Portland, OR: Microcosm, 2005.

Burch, David. *Fundamentals of Kayak Navigation, 4th: Master the Traditional Skills and the Latest Technologies.* Guilford, CT: Falcon, 2008.

Greenlaw, Linda. *The Hungry Ocean: A Swordboat Captain's Journey.* New York, NY: Hyperion, 2006.

Limeres, René, ed. *Alaska Fishing: The Ultimate Angler's Guide.* Third edition. Roseville, CA: Publishers Design Group, 2005.

McCloskey, William. *Breakers: A Novel About the Commercial Fishermen of Alaska.* New York, NY: The Lyons Press, 2004.

Molyneaux, Paul. *The Doryman's Reflection: A Fisherman's Life.* New York, NY: Thunders Mouth Press, 2005.

Peluso, Charles, and Sandy MacFarlane. *Tiggie: The Lure and Lore of Commercial Fishing in New England.* Bloomington, IN: Rooftop Publishing, 2007.

Pollizotto, Martin. *Saltwater Fishing Made Easy.* New York, NY: International Marine/Ragged Mountain Press, 2006.

Prybot, Peter K. *Lobstering Off Cape Ann: A Lifetime Lobsterman Remembers.* Charleston, SC: The History Press, 2006.

Seavey, Wendell. *Working the Sea: Misadventures, Ghost Stories, and Life Lessons from a Maine Lobster Fisherman.* Berkeley, CA: North Atlantic Books, 2005.

Stuhaug, Dennis. *The Complete Idiot's Guide to Canoeing and Kayaking.* New York, NY: Alpha, 2004.

Stuhaug, Dennis. *Kayaking Made Easy, 3rd: A Manual for Beginners with Tips for the Experienced* (Made Easy Series). Guilford, CT: Falcon, 2006.

Underwood, Lamar, ed. *The Greatest Fishing Stories Ever Told: Twenty-Eight Unforgettable Fishing Tales.* First edition. Guilford, CT: The Lyons Press, 2004.

MAGAZINES

Alaska Fisherman's Journal
http://www.afjournal.com

Aquaculture Magazine
http://www.aquaculturemag.com

Boats and Harbors: The Commercial Marine Marketplace
http://www.boats-and-harbors.com

Commercial Fisheries News
http://www.fish-news.com

The Fishermen's News
http://www.fishermensnews.com

Fish Farming News
http://www.fish-news.com/ffn.htm

Marine Yellow Pages
http://www.marineyellowpages.com

National Fisherman
http://www.nationalfisherman.com
This commercial fishing news site includes blogs kept by fishers and an at-sea diary.

Pacific Fishing
http://www.pacificfishing.com
The West Coast's leading commercial fishing magazine.

Streaming Fish Videos
http://www.FishingWorks.com/FishingWorks.cfm?page=CL_detail.
    cfm&category_id=921&part_id=5
Streaming videos on the art of fishing.

World Fishing
http://www.worldfishing.net

VIDEOS

Alaska the Great State of Commercial Fishing (2000)
Ydot.com.

FISHING WEBCAMS

http://www.fishingworks.com/fishing-webcams

3

RANCH HAND

If you love farms, horses, and working outdoors, and have an easy-going, sociable personality, you might be cut out to be a professional ranch hand. You may fear that this is more a Hollywood fantasy than a real job, but there are lots of opportunities to work as a wrangler at either a working, family-owned cattle ranch or a dude ranch (a ranch that is open to vacationers). If you are hoping to spend your workday in some of the most majestic places in the world, look no further.

Description

The basic duties of a ranch hand—or wrangler—on a working ranch are tending livestock and repairing and cleaning fences, ranch buildings, and equipment. Tending livestock usually includes feeding, birthing, branding, shearing, roping, sorting, pasturing, herding, grooming, and doctoring the ranch's horses, cattle, poultry, pigs, and/or sheep. Having raised healthy animals through this attentive care, ranch hands must also haul the livestock to market or to a shipping terminal.

Horses are particularly crucial to the operation of a successful ranch, regardless of whether it is a working or a dude ranch. It falls to the wranglers to care for the horses on the ranch. At a working ranch, horses are used to herd cattle. At a dude ranch, the horses are usually younger and are used for taking guests riding. Because of this, their health and well-being are very important. Horse-related duties include daily brushing and grooming, tack and equipment upkeep and repair, basic veterinarian skills, fence building and repair, trail maintenance, and the maintenance and cleaning of corrals.

Wrangler jobs on dude ranches require not only considerable skill in horsemanship and stable operation but also

A wrangler herds horses on a ranch.

good people skills, as you must be able to interact with adult guests and their children. Many ranches have access to private water sources, offering fishing opportunities as well. A good ranch guide may also be expected to take guests on overnight hiking and fishing trips or cattle drives, teach basic riding skills, lead horseback riding and river rafting expeditions, and perhaps get behind the wheel for some off-road, four-wheel drive adventures. Jobs on dude ranches generally involve lots of hard work, long hours (usually dawn to dusk), and participation in evening activities for guests, such as line

Guests practice lassoing at the Teton Valley Ranch Camp in Jackson Hole, Wyoming.

dances, cookouts, hayrides, and staff talent shows. Most northern dude ranches hire their hands during the period between November and April. Southern dude ranches hire in the August to October season. While pay is usually low, compensation often includes room and board, a share of tips, and use of the facilities and horses when off duty.

Education/Training

You don't need a formal education to succeed in this line of work; hands-on experience is the best schooling.

The History of Dude Ranching

Dude ranching first emerged in the late 1800s when European visitors and American tourists from the East first began to travel out West. These ranches provided safe, comfortable accommodations in beautiful and rugged settings, and gave guests a taste of what ranch life was really like. For a fee of ten dollars, guests received a full week of accommodations, hearty meals, horses to ride, and the company of ranchers. Modern-day dude ranches offer the very same pleasures (though at a higher rate).

Fortunately, seasonal work is pretty easy to come by. If you hope someday to advance to ranch foreman or even own your own ranch, you should consider a community college or university degree in agricultural production, agricultural economics, animal husbandry, or veterinary medicine. Other ranch jobs to consider as a starting point include children's counselor, trails foreman, groomer, cook, wait-staff member, maintenance worker, or, in the winter months, cross-country ski instructor. Trails foremen are usually required to have a background in trail planning and building. Aside from previous work experience, the only official training you should look into getting for most of these jobs is CPR and first-aid certification.

Outlook

With dude ranches becoming an increasingly popular destination for families seeking a unique vacation, there are growing opportunities in this field. In addition, many western states, such as Texas and Wyoming, have reported shortages of ranch hands in recent years. Working ranches and cattle outfits may hire interns to train as ranch hands.

You have many geographic options if you wish to pursue employment as a ranch hand. Try Arizona, California, Colorado, Montana, Nevada, New Mexico, New York, Texas, Washington, Wyoming, or Hawaii. In Canada, you can try Alberta and British Columbia. And don't forget Mexico, Argentina, Brazil, and other ranch-friendly areas.

FOR MORE INFORMATION

ASSOCIATIONS

Alberta Country Vacation Association
Box 396
Sangudo, AB T0E 2A0
Canada
(403) 785-3700
http://www.albertacountryvacation.com

Arizona Dude Ranch Association
P.O. Box 603K
Cortaro, AZ 85625
http://www.azdra.com

British Columbia Guest Ranch Association
P.O. Box 3301
Kamloops, BC V2C 6B9
Canada
(250) 374-6836
http://www.bcguestranches.com

Colorado Dude and Guest Ranch Association
P.O. Box 2120
Granby, CO 80446
(970) 887-3128
http://www.coloradoranch.com

The Dude Ranchers' Association
P.O. Box 741K
LaPorte, CO 80535
(970) 223-8440
http://www.duderanch.org

Idaho Guest and Dude Ranch Association
HC 72 K
Cascade, ID 83611
(208) 382-4336

Montana Big Sky Ranch Association
1627 West Main Street, Suite 434K
Bozeman, MT 59715

Texas Guest Ranch Association
900 Congress Avenue, Suite 201
Austin, TX 78701
(512) 474-2996

WEB SITES

Dude Ranch and Guest Ranch Headquarters
http://www.ranchweb.com
Dude Ranch Jobs
http://www.duderanchjobs.com

Gene Kilgore's Online Guide to Ranch Vacations
http://www.ranchweb.com/multimedia.htm

National Cowgirl Museum and Hall of Fame
http://www.cowgirl.net

Summer Jobs at Dude Ranches and Guest Ranches
http://www.coolworks.com/ranch_jobs.htm

VIDEOS/DVDS

Dude Ranch Days (1999)
PBS Home Video.

Dude Ranches Out West: Then and Now (1997)
Tapeworm.

BOOKS

Evans, Max. *Making a Hand: Growing Up Cowboy in New Mexico*. Santa Fe, NM: Museum of New Mexico Press, 2005.

McClellan, Doris, and Elmer Kelton. *Cowboys Cowgirls Cowchips: True Tales from Long X, Long S & Spade Ranches*. Albany, TX: Bright Sky Press, 2005.

O'Byrne, Tim. *Cowboys & Buckaroos: Trade Secrets of a North American Icon*. Colorado Springs, CO: Western Horseman, 2005.

White, Courtney. *Revolution on the Range: The Rise of a New Ranch in the American West*. Washington, DC: Island Press, 2008.

MAGAZINES

Cowboy Magazine
http://www.cowboymagazine.com

4

ECOTOURISM PLANNER

Ecotourism is fairly new. The term refers to trips to exotic or remote locales that are not often frequented by tourists, such as the Arctic Circle or Brazilian rain forests. The real key to ecotours, though, is that while the adventure should enrich the traveler, it must not damage the ecosystem of the place being visited, and it should be economically beneficial to the local people.

This is the right time to be getting into ecotourism. Every year the industry grows significantly, and 2002 was declared the International Year of Ecotourism by the United Nations. According to an article in *Green Money Journal*, ecotourism is a $77 billion market, while a Travel Industry of America survey estimated that over 55 million U.S. travelers can be classified as "geo-tourists" who are interested in nature, culture, and heritage tourism. As ecotours continue to grow in popularity with adventurous and thoughtful travelers worldwide, the employment opportunities within the industry for people who want to lead or organize tours in wild and uncharted places become ever greater.

Description

To be successful in this field, you will need good communication skills, the ability to work independently and creatively, and a sense of adventure. Although you do not need to go to school to prepare, you should be willing to do lots of your own research, both through reading and by visiting the places where you someday wish to lead tours. Once you are well informed and are knowledgeable in your chosen area of expertise, you can begin guiding ecotours for an established and reputable ecotour operator or even start your own company.

Tourism is the world's largest industry, and according to the UN's World Tourism Organization, in 2004 ecotourism

Students listen to a guide explain buttress roots in a rain forest at Yacumama Lodge in Iquitos, Peru.

and nature tourism grew three times faster than the tourism industry as a whole. For an increasing number of countries, tourism based on natural attractions is the leading source of national revenue. As a result, ecotourism is promoted more every year, and its economic importance has grown in equal measure. Because people are now realizing that there is money to be made in this field, ecotourism has given governments and local residents powerful incentives to conserve natural and cultural resources. Often, a happy by-product of ecotourism is the development and enrichment of communities that have traditionally been impoverished. For all these reasons, many individuals, organizations, and governments are getting behind ecotourism. As a result, there are many new opportunities for an adventurous person to launch a career in ecotourism, allowing her or him a chance to make a good living, see the world, and work toward a good cause—ecological conservation and community development.

As an ecotravel guide or tour operator, there are several principles and practices you would be expected to adopt. You must develop an understanding of and respect for the complex interactions of plants, animals, and humans. As a guide, you must be knowledgeable and entertaining, and be able to transform hard science and ancient history into accessible, interesting talks. You should try to involve local people as much as possible in your tours and encourage your travelers to support local businesses. As well, you should fill as many job positions as possible with local employees who ordinarily have very limited economic opportunities. In this way, local residents will clearly see the value of preserving their environment and the travelers you lead will learn about the customs, traditions, and languages of their hosts. Above all, you should avoid or minimize any environmental harm to fragile ecosystems and encourage your travelers to join organizations that support preservation and protect the rights of indigenous peoples around the world.

Street vendors tend to their fare at a local market in Antigua, Guatemala.

Education/Training

Robert Smith, owner of the ecotour company Timbuktours, advises getting a background in first aid, natural interpretation, and other basic skills before embarking on a career in ecotourism. He believes that getting a degree is not necessary and that a few background courses are more than enough.

"Many secondary education institutions and universities offer short-term courses and certification programs that apply directly to the eco- and adventure tourism industry," he says.

The International Ecotourism Society (TIES) offers training in this field in the form of forums, field seminars, and workshops. Park rangers, landscape architects, and other nature professionals from dozens of countries around the globe attend its events.

Profile

Robert Smith, ecotour guide
Owner, Timbuktours

WHY IS ECOTOURISM SO POPULAR?

With so many frontiers in a rapidly developing market, the time to take advantage of these opportunities would be now, while regulation is more or lcss wide open. Because many people are increasingly feeling a need to interact with the natural environment, ecotourism will become more and more popular.

HOW DID YOU GET INVOLVED IN THIS UNIQUE INDUSTRY?

I've been a guide ever since I can remember, venturing alone or with friends into the bush in my native South Africa. Alone, I was guided by my instincts, intuition, and knowledge, and I was usually the appointed leader when venturing outdoors. My know-how, or bushwhacking ability, was first gained by being a Boy Scout as a youth, and later as an infantryman in the military. I also learned a lot from an uncle who was a nature conservationist.

WHY DID YOU START YOUR OWN COMPANY?

Because of the understanding I have of the natural world, I am definitely in favor of "treading lightly" and the "leave no trace" protocol. This explains my affiliation with eco-tourism, which allows people to get closer to the environment with much less intrusion than conventional forms of tourism.

Today I operate as an eco/adventure guide and wilderness interpreter in the Republic of South Africa, Canada, and in other countries. With hiking, camping, ocean kayaking, and river rafting as my means for giving my clients the kind of travel experience they will never forget, I have created the opportunity for myself to work and play hard simultaneously.

WHAT ADVICE COULD YOU GIVE YOUNG PEOPLE WHO SHARE YOUR INTERESTS?

If you are the same kind of person as I am, then ecotourism is your ticket to a rewarding career. Many people finish high school and do not have a very clear realization of what they intend to do with their lives afterwards. After all, this is a rather big decision to make. There are not many alternatives to the rat race. However, with the rapid and large-scale expansion of tourism, there are some opportunities to be found.

FOR MORE INFORMATION

ASSOCIATIONS

Conservation International

1919 M Street NW
Suite 600
Washington, DC 20036
(202) 912-1000
(800) 406-2306
d.vizcaino@conservation.org
http://www.conservation.org
http://www.ecotour.org (Eco Tourism International at Conservation
    International)

Earthwatch Institute International Headquarters

3 Clock Tower Place, Suite 100
Box 75
Maynard, MA 01754
(800) 776-0188
info@earthwatch.org
http://www.earthwatch.org

Ecoventura/Galapagos Network

6303 Blue Lagoon Drive, Suite 140
Miami, FL 33126
(305) 262-6264
(800) 633-7972
info@galapagosnetwork.com
http://www.ecoventura.com

International Ecotourism Club
P.O. Box 65232
Psihico, 15410
Athens, Greece
+30 1 671 9671
a@ecoclub.com
http://www.ecoclub.com

The International Ecotourism Society
1333 H St., NW
Suite 300, East Tower
Washington, DC 20005
(202) 347-9203
info@ecotourism.org
http://www.ecotourism.org

Manaca, Inc.
1609 Connecticut Avenue NW
4th Floor
Washington, DC 20009
(202) 265-8204
andreas@manaca.com
http://www.manaca.com

Programme for Belize
1 Eyre Street
Belize City, Belize
(501) 275 616
pfbel@btl.net
http://www.pfbelize.org

Responsibletravel.com
3rd floor, Pavilion House
6 Old Steine
Brighton BN1 1EJ
UK

+44 (0)1273 600030
amelia@responsibletravel.com
http://www.responsibletravel.com

Turismo da Natureza Portugal
Av. Eng. Arantes e Oliveira n. 13, 4 B
Lisboa, 1900-221 Portugal
+351 21 841 8743
ui.marques@icat.fc.ul.pt
http://www.icat.fc.ul.pt

World Travel & Tourism Council
1-2 Queen Victoria Terrace
Sovereign Court
London E1W 3HA
United Kingdom
44 (0)870 727 9882
enquiries@wttc.org
http://www.wttc.org

PROGRAMS

The International Ecotourism Society (TIES) Training Opportunities
TIES offers specialized programs in coordination with:
• University-based programs: For training partnerships with universities, TIES is generally responsible for curriculum development and course implementation, while the university coordinates publicity and registration for the course.
• Government and NGO-sponsored programs: TIES designs curricula that can be used as part of ecotourism training programs for host governments and non-government organizations (NGOs) interested in upgrading the skills of local professionals in the field of ecotourism.
• Private-sector sponsored programs: TIES provides tailored training programs to the personnel of specific tourism companies.

WEB SITES

Ecotourism electronic newsletter
http://ecotourism.cc/r/news.html

Ecotourism news
http://ecotourism.cc

Ecotourism Travel Guide
http://www.ecotourismlogue.com

Guide to EcoTravel
http://www.naturalist.com/channels/Ecotravel

International Ecotourism Society
http://www.ecotourism.org

Lindblad Expeditions: Adventure Travel
http://www.expeditions.com

Nature Travel EcoVolunteer
http://www.ecovolunteer.org
A travel agency that arranges trips for tourists who want to work with local organizations' conservation projects.

Responsible Tourism Partnership
http://www.responsibletourismpartnership.org

BOOKS

Fritsch, Al, and Kristin Johannsen. *Ecotourism in Appalachia: Marketing the Mountains*. Lexington, KY: The University Press of Kentucky, 2004.

Fuad-Luke, Alastair. *The Eco-Travel Guide*. New York, NY: Thames & Hudson, 2008.

Hood, Mary A. *RiverTime: Ecotravel on the World's Rivers*. Albany, NY: State University of New York Press, 2008.

Mitchell, G. *How to Start a Tour Guiding Business*. Third edition. Charleston, SC: The GEM Group, 2005.

Robinson, Hannah. *Australia: An Ecotraveler's Guide*. Northampton, MA: Interlink Publishing Group, 2004.

Weaver, David. *Sustainable Tourism*. Burlington, MA: Elsevier, 2006.

MULTIMEDIA

Honey, Martha. "The Business of EcoTourism."
http://www.greenmoneyjournal.com/article.mpl?newsletterid=37&articleid=467

Shum, Katrina. "Green Travel: Trends in Ecotourism."
http://www.lohas.com/journal/ecotourism.htm

5

GROUNDSKEEPER

Groundskeeping is a kind of urban or suburban safari. The work is varied, physically demanding, always changing, and tremendously gratifying for those who enjoy being outside and leaving their environment better off than when they found it. Considerable physical activity in all sorts of weather makes the work as challenging as it is rewarding.

Description

According to the Professional Lawn Care Association of America (PLCAA), lawn and landscape maintenance is the number one "green industry" service. Groundskeepers or landscapers are responsible for designing and maintaining healthy lawns and gardens. They maintain the grounds of industrial, commercial, or public property (such as parks and botanical gardens). They may also maintain a variety of facilities, including athletic fields, golf courses, and cemeteries. In addition, some groundskeepers are responsible for indoor greenery, such as the lush environments often found in malls, hotels, and interior exhibits in botanical gardens. Groundskeepers perform all facets of grounds work, such as mowing, raking, trimming, landscaping, sod laying, watering, fertilizing, digging, and gardening. To help them perform these tasks, they use hand tools such as shovels, rakes, pruning shears, saws, and hedge clippers. They also operate a variety of power equipment, including riding mowers, snowblowers, chain saws, loaders, tractors, and field marking equipment.

Many landscaping and groundskeeping jobs are seasonal. Demand for grounds work is greatest in spring, summer, and fall. Most of this work is performed outdoors and, because of all the digging of holes, lifting of young trees, and pushing of heavy machinery, requires a lot of strength and stamina.

The design and maintenance of lawns and gardens sometimes involves topiary art—cutting and trimming trees into original or ornamental shapes.

Most entry-level jobs in the industry require no college education; in fact, almost half of new hires do not yet have a high school diploma. Instead, training in landscaping techniques and the use of mowers, trimmers, leaf blowers, and tractors occurs on the job. Wages tend to be low (entry-level landscaping and groundskeeping laborers receive an average of $10.75 an hour, according to the U.S. Department of Labor's 2006 statistics), but for nature lovers the paycheck is offset by the days spent outside, the varied workday, and the satisfaction of participating in the beautification of one's surroundings.

Nursery and greenhouse workers grow the plants, flowers, shrubs, and trees that will eventually be planted by landscapers. Landscape contractors turn the designs of landscape architects into reality. They supervise the planting of trees, shrubs, and flowers; the laying of sod; and the placement of benches, statuary, and other design elements. They may also install lighting and sprinkler systems and build footpaths, patios, decks, and fountains. They may work only on large commercial projects, such as office complexes, corporate parks, and malls, or they may offer their services to private residences. The landscape contractor directs a supervisor who in turn oversees the landscape laborers who actually perform all the grounds work.

Groundskeeping laborers tend to focus on the maintenance of facilities, such as playing fields, golf courses, parks, college campuses, and cemeteries. Their duties are often identical to those of landscape laborers but may also include clearing snow from walkways and parking lots; maintaining and repairing sidewalks, planters, fountains, pools, fences, and benches; turf care and painting; and, in the case of cemetery laborers, digging graves with a backhoe and preparing and maintaining burial plots.

Seeing the result of his or her work is perhaps one of the most rewarding benefits of a groundskeeper's job.

Education/Training

Typically, groundskeepers must have a high school diploma (or the equivalent) and a driver's license, and should be able to demonstrate literacy and good interpersonal skills. The best education is the one you get by observing more experienced workers on the job and by getting your hands dirty. You will learn skills like planting, cultivating, and pruning trees, and fertilizing lawns, trees, and shrubs, as

Hello, Sports Fans!

One major segment of the groundskeeping industry is tending to the very particular needs of athletic fields, especially those used by professional athletes. This includes the grounds that football, baseball, golf, and tennis are played on. The grass or turf must be perfectly maintained and properly drained through the use of tractors, aerators, fertilizers, and insecticides. Astroturf must be vacuumed and disinfected. Groundskeepers who care for athletic fields keep natural and artificial turf fields in top condition, mark out boundaries, and paint turf with team logos and names before events take place. Workers who maintain golf courses are called greenskeepers. They do many of the same things other grounds-keepers do, but they may also relocate the holes on putting greens and repair and paint ball washers, benches, and tee markers. Imagine the satisfaction of seeing your handiwork on television while your favorite team plays on the field you have tended with such care!

well as how to operate equipment. Inexpensive courses in gardening and horticulture are often available at nurseries and greenhouses, and will provide a solid background for your career.

Many high school and two-year vocational/technical school graduates as well as retirees are entering this field, according to the PLCAA. The American Society of Landscape Architects' (ASLA) National Certification Program offers exams and certification for landscape professionals.

Outlook

Every landowning entity (including corporations, amusement parks, professional sports organizations, the government, public institutions like schools and universities, home owners, apartment complexes, and city parks) has a need for beautification and the upkeep of its grounds. Demand is increasing for landscaping and groundskeeping services as construction of commercial and industrial complexes, homes, parks, and highways has continued to grow. In addition, turnover among landscapers and groundskeepers is high, so it is usually easy to find an entry-level job. This means groundskeepers can find satisfying work in just about any location: urban, rural, or suburban. You can work as part of the groundskeeping staff at a large institution, for a private contractor, or even go into business for yourself.

FOR MORE INFORMATION

ASSOCIATIONS

American Landscape Maintenance Association
737 Hollywood Boulevard
Hollywood, FL 33019
(954) 927-3100
http://www.floridalma.org/OrgLinks.htm

American Nursery and Landscape Association
1250 I Street NW, Suite 500
Washington, DC 20005-3922
(202) 789-2900
http://www.anla.org

American Society of Agronomy
677 South Segoe Road
Madison, WI 53711
(608) 273-8080
headquarters@agronomy.org
http://www.agronomy.org

American Society of Landscape Architects
908 North Second Street
Harrisburg, PA 17102
(717) 236-2044
http://www.landscapearchitects.org

Associated Landscape Contractors of America, Inc.
150 Elden Street, Suite 270
Herndon, VA 20170
http://www.alca.org

California Landscape & Irrigation Council Inc.
4195 Chino Hills Parkway
Suite 398
Chino Hills, CA 91709
(909) 393-2114
clic@att.net
http://www.cliccontractors.com/home.html

Canadian Nursery Landscape Association
Grounds Maintenance for golf and green industry professionals
http://www.grounds-mag.com/associations

Landscape Contractors Association of MD-DC-VA
15245 Shady Grove Road, Suite 130
Rockville, MD 20850
(301) 948-0810
lca@mgmtsol.com
http://www.lcamddcva.org

National Institute on Park & Grounds Management
730 W. Frances Street
Appleton, WI 54914-2365
ipgm@tpo.org

National Recreation & Park Association
22377 Belmont Ridge Road
Ashburn, VA 20148
(540) 858-0784
(800) 626-6772
info@nrpa.org
http://www.nrpa.org

Professional Grounds Management Society
720 Light Street
Baltimore, MD 21230
(800) 609-7467
http://www.pgms.org

Sports Turf Managers Association
1375 Rolling Hills Loop
Council Bluffs, IA 51503-8552
(800) 323-3875
http://www.stma.org

Turf and Ornamental Communicators Association (TOCA)
120 W. Main Street
P.O. Box 156
New Prague, MN 56071
(612) 758-6340
http://www.toca.org

WEB SITES

Groundskeeper University
http://www.groundskeeper.com

LandscapcOnline
http://www.landscapeonline.com

***Plant Healthcare* online magazine**
http://www.planthealthcare.com

MAGAZINES

Landscape Management: Solutions for a Growing Industry
http://www.landscapemanagement.net

Lawn and Landscape Magazine
http://www.lawnandlandscape.com

BOOKS

Bradley, Steve. *The Pruner's Bible: A Step-by-Step Guide to Pruning Every Plant in Your Garden*. London, England: Quarto Publishing, 2005.

Dell, Owen. *How to Start a Home-Based Landscaping Business* (Home-Based Business Series). Guilford, CT: Globe Pequot, 2005.

Hampshire, Kristen. *John Deere Landscaping & Lawn Care: The Complete Guide to a Beautiful Yard Year-Round*. Gloucester, MA: Quarry Books, 2007.

LaRusic, Joel. *Start & Run A Landscaping Business*. Bellingham, WA: Self-Counsel Press, 2005.

Rogers, Trey. *Lawn Geek: Tips and Tricks for the Ultimate Turf from the Guru of Grass*. New York, NY: NAL Trade, 2007.

Sorvig, Kim, and J. William Thompson. *Sustainable Landscape Construction: A Guide to Green Building Outdoors*. Second edition. Washington, DC: Island Press, 2007.

TEACHER/
NATURALIST

Though close observation of nature is as old as humanity itself, the methodical, codified system of its study that we use today is less than 300 years old. The formal study of nature that was created and adopted by scientists and amateur science enthusiasts, who became known as naturalists, began in England with the Reverend Gilbert White, who was born in 1720. Today the term "naturalist" has several meanings. Teacher/naturalists are community outreach leaders, educators, nature experts, writers, and explorers, all rolled into one. Although some positions require naturalists to hold an advanced degree, there are many opportunities for self-education and advancement through hands-on experience in this fascinating and rewarding career.

Description

Often, the title of this job is "teacher/naturalist" or "instructor/naturalist." This type of job is most commonly found at nature centers or preservation associations. You may also find employment at zoos, zoological gardens, or summer camps. Naturalists provide natural science programs to schools, interested groups, and the general public. Most teacher/naturalists fulfill many functions during the course of a single workday; their job requires them to serve as writers (of articles, brochures, and explanatory text on walls or posted near trails), teachers, historians, and mentors. They often lead field trips for visiting schoolchildren and deliver presentations in schools. Naturalists plan, organize, and conduct bird-watching expeditions, nature walks, seminars on outdoor skills, and nature-inspired craft classes. They can even get involved in land-use decisions concerning the parks in which they work; their opinion may be sought on what trees

Hikers walk up a steep path in the Sacred Valley of the Incas in Peru.

should be cut, how and where trails should be constructed, and where and if additional campsites should be built.

Because there is very little money to be made as a teacher/naturalist, you must have a genuine love for nature, its study, and its enjoyment. You should have a real curiosity about the natural world and how it works and a real desire to share what you learn with others. Needless to say, you should be physically fit and active. Having a sense of creativity and initiative is also useful; this will make the programs you create, the articles and interpretive texts you write, and the talks you deliver far more interesting and informative to a wide audience. You will also have to be flexible. You will often have to work on weekends and at night (when most of the public finally has time for camping, hiking, biking, and stargazing). Naturalist jobs are not very plentiful, so you should be prepared to relocate if necessary.

Education/Training

As positions vary in this field, so do qualification requirements. For example, naturalists at the New Jersey Audubon Society (NJAS) are required to have some knowledge of natural history, a background in education, excellent communication and time-management skills, and a cooperative attitude. NJAS believes that for a naturalist position, field experience is more valuable than a degree in natural science, and the necessary formal education can be attained through many of its own projects and not-for-credit workshops. Internships are another great way to gain hands-on experience in this field. Many nature centers and zoos employ interns to provide opportunities for individuals to gain experience in the field of natural science. Working as an intern or volunteering at a park, nature center, zoo, museum, or camp can be useful training and may eventually lead to a paying job. Some high schools, such as North

A naturalist sets up a naked mole rat exhibit at the Burnet Park Zoo in Syracuse, New York.

Hollywood High School in Los Angeles, California, and the High School for Environmental Studies in New York City, offer a program of classes on ecology. These classes cover agriculture, environmental science, Latin, personal and planetary health, ecology, systems theory, economics, and botany. It is a very good idea to take some environmental studies courses that are offered at your local community college. The more formal education you have, the more employable you will be.

Aside from formal academic training and the hands-on experience offered by internships and volunteer positions, you can do much to educate yourself in the wonders of the natural world. Explore your own neighborhood and town. Study its natural features, green spaces, wildlife, and vegetation. Go to the library to study the area's natural history; research will be an important component of your work as a teacher/naturalist, so it is a good idea to develop these skills. Always carry a sketchbook with you so you can record any interesting or unusual flowers, birds, leaves, or land features you may encounter. This will help sharpen your observation skills, which will someday be of great importance in your job.

Profile

Jenny Case, community outreach coordinator for the Nature Conservancy

HOW DID YOU GET INVOLVED IN WORKING WITH NATURE?
Nature is where my heart lies. My first interest was plants. I studied some biology and worked in greenhouses and fruit and dairy farms. We see a lot of birds and many plant varieties on our nature walks, and my background in identifying different plants has been helpful.

When I began my job search, I had two small children and needed something with flexible hours. When I saw the ad for this job with the Nature Conservancy, I was thrilled.

IS THIS YOUR FIRST EXPERIENCE WORKING WITH NATURE?

No. In fact, because I was already active in the outdoors and knew about planning trips from working in the recreation industry, I was a good match for this job.

WHY DOES THE NATURE CONSERVANCY DO COMMUNITY OUTREACH?

As an organization, we are looking for compatible ways to conserve natural resources and land. We were losing land and species at an alarming rate, and in order to accomplish our mission, we needed to do more outreach and education for the public.

DESCRIBE YOUR NORMAL DAY.

There is no one type of day for me! That's what I love. I have a lot of variety in my job. But in general I plan seasonal schedules. For instance, I will plot out three months at a time by supplementing our old standby activities, like hiking to the waterfall, with newer ideas. Some of the other activities I'm excited about are stargazing evenings, a summer solstice event hosted by a Native American couple, and book readings by famous naturalists and authors. That kind of thing.

FOR MORE INFORMATION

ASSOCIATIONS/CLUBS

American Birding Association
P.O. Box 6599
Colorado Springs, CO 80934
(719) 578-9703
member@aba.org
http://www.americanbirding.org

American Ornithologists Union
c/o Division of Birds MRC 116
National Museum of Natural History
Washington, DC 20560
aou@nmnh.si.edu
http://www.aou.org

Appalachian Studies Association
Regional Research Institute—WVU
P.O. Box 6825
Morgantown, WV 26506
(304) 293-8541
RRIASA@wvnvm.wvnet.edu
http://www.appalachianstudies.org

Becoming an Outdoors-Woman (BOW)
(877) BOWOMAN (269-6626)
peggy.farrell@uwsp.edu
http://www.uwsp.edu/CNR/bow

Young Naturalist Company
1900 North Main
North Newton, KS 67117

(316) 283-4103
oungnat@southwind.net
http://www.youngnaturalistcompany.com

WEB SITES

American Society of Naturalists
http://www.amnat.org

Audubon Naturalist Society
http://www.audubonnaturalist.org

Mountain Nature
http://www.mountainnature.com/10_secrets_to_becoming_an_
expert.htm
Check out tips on becoming a naturalist from Ward Cameron, naturalist, author, and storyteller.

A Naturalist's World
http://www.tracknature.com
Nonprofit e-zine focusing on personal stories concerning environmental causes and exploration.

BOOKS

Baker, Nick. *Amateur Naturalist*. Washington, DC: National Geographic, 2005.

Huxley, Robert, ed. *The Great Naturalists*. London, England: Thames & Hudson, 2007.

Kirkland, Jane. *No Student Left Indoors: Creating a Field Guide to Your Schoolyard* (Take a Walk series). Lionville, PA: Stillwater Publishing, 2007.

Leslie, Clare Walker. *Into the Field: A Guide to Locally Focused Teaching* (Nature Literacy Series Vol. 3). Great Barrington, MA: Orion Society, 2005.

Rhinehart, Kurt. *Naturalist's Guide to Observing Nature*. Mechanicsburg, PA: Stackpole Books, 2006.

Schaller, George B. *A Naturalist and Other Beasts: Tales from a Life in the Field*. San Francisco, CA: Sierra Club Books, 2007.

JOURNALS AND MAGAZINES

American Midland Naturalist
P.O. Box 369
Notre Dame, IN 46556-0369
(219) 631-7481
ammidnat.1@nd.edu

The American Naturalist
http://www.journals.uchicago.edu/AN/home.html

Birding Magazine, American Birding
http://www.americanbirding.org/pubs/birding/index.html

Refuge Reporter
Avocet Crossing
Millwood, VA 22646-0156
(540) 837-2152
refrep@mnsinc.com

WildBird Magazine
Fancy Publications, Inc.
P.O. Box 6050
Mission Viejo, CA 92690
(714) 855-8822
A magazine dedicated to bird-watching.

Wilderness Way
P.O. Box 203
Lufkin, TX 75904-0203
(409) 632-8746
This magazine covers many topics: survival skills, outdoor activities, primitive and historical ways of life, culture, earth medicine, and Native American studies.

VIDEOS/DVDS

The Naturalist, Kent Bonar (2001)
High Plains Films.

MULTIMEDIA

Nature Blog Network
http://natureblognetwork.com
A directory of blogs about nature study.

Nature.com
http://www.nature.com/nature/multimedia
The classic magazine of nature and science has a Web site with
    blogs, videos, and podcasts.

90 Second Naturalist (Web radio show)
http://www.nsnaturalist.org

[7]

PARK RANGER

For those of you who love to be out-doors, there is likely no better career path than the one that leads to the National Park Service (NPS). With at least one national park in every state in the United States (and many in Canada), park rangers have a thrilling variety of experiences waiting for them in the wild.

Description

The mission of the National Park Service is to "conserve the scenery and the natural and historic objects and the wildlife therein, and to provide for the enjoyment of the same in such manner and by such means as will leave them unimpaired for the enjoyment of future generations." If you are committed to the mission of both preserving nature and providing the public with an opportunity to appreciate and enjoy it, you will fit in perfectly at the National Park Service. Ranger jobs involve equal parts conservation and public relations. The duties are very wide-ranging, ensuring that each new work-day will be a little different than the last. On any given day, you may find yourself preparing exhibits and informational material; developing recreational activities and conservation programs; leading tours and nature walks; presenting educational talks to visitors; demonstrating folk arts and crafts; working on conservation, habitat restoration, and ecological projects; studying wildlife behavior; monitoring air and water quality in the park; searching for lost hikers and campers; rescuing stranded climbers; fighting fires; transporting injured park guests to hospitals; administering first aid; and serving as a law enforcement officer.

Working conditions vary depending on the location of your park. National parks are located in forests, deserts, mountain ranges, wetlands, coastal regions, and even big cities. Much of your day will probably be spent outside, exposed to the elements and weather patterns associated with these types of terrain.

Education/Training

A college degree can mean a higher salary, although in some cases work experience can serve as a substitute for education. Field experience is very valuable and will set you apart from other high school graduates. You can volunteer or intern at a nature center, outdoor education center, or state or national park to get experience in the field and find out which duties or geographic areas you prefer. Try contacting your local forester, wildlife manager, or naturalist to inquire about such opportunities.

Many park rangers break into entry-level positions after high school, beginning their careers as seasonal rangers (or as volunteers). Seasonal rangers either work in one park for part of the year or travel from park to park, working at one in the winter and another in the summer. They usually perform the ranger equivalent of grunt work, such as toll collecting, cleaning campsites, maintaining trails, staffing information desks, and guiding tours. They receive few if any benefits. You may have to work as a seasonal ranger for several years before a full-time position becomes available. Once you win this job, however, you will enjoy good job

National Park Service park rangers examine wildlife in a pond in Smithfield, Rhode Island.

security and greater stability. Most full-time park rangers remain at the same park for many years.

The orientation and training a ranger receives on the job is sometimes supplemented with formal training courses. Training for duties that are unique to the National Park Service is available at the Horace M. Albright Training Center at Grand Canyon National Park, Arizona, and at the Stephen T. Mather Training Center at Harpers Ferry, West Virginia. It is also a good idea to take courses in environmental sciences, park management, natural history, forestry, outdoor recreation, and/or communications during seasonal layoffs. The more formal education you can combine with real-world experience, the better your chances of landing a full-time ranger position. You may want to be aware, however, that some park ranger positions do require a bachelor's degree, while a master's degree is helpful for those hoping to become supervisors and managers.

Those interested in park ranger jobs (at city, county, state, or national parks) should apply at county, city, special district personnel, and regional offices of the National Park Service.

Outlook

Most park rangers will advise you to be willing to go where the jobs are. The largest number are in urban areas, but with a little experience, you will be more likely to be able to pick a region in which you most want to work. The experience gained from seasonal work is directly applicable to advancement to permanent positions.

Though highly prized, full-time ranger positions do not pay very well. Since this is a government job, full-time rangers receive a complete benefits package, which includes overtime, paid vacations, holidays, sick leave, health insurance, and retirement benefits. In some cases, rangers live in government-provided housing within the

City Slickers

A park ranger places a small cage over a turtle's nest in Dania Beach, Florida, to prevent the expected hatchlings from crawling into oil patches on the beach.

The popular image of a park ranger is someone who works in a remote forest or high atop a mountain out west. You may be surprised to learn that park rangers can also work in urban and suburban areas. According to the NPS, more than half of all rangers work in areas east of the Mississippi River. Most of your job will take place outdoors, but you may do some office work if you move into a management position. During your career, you are likely to be assigned to several different parts of the country. Depending upon qualifications, park rangers begin their service at various grades, and salary increases along with rank.

park. Most rangers feel the low pay is more than offset by the love they feel for their work and their surroundings.

FOR MORE INFORMATION

NATIONAL PARKS AND MONUMENTS

Acadia, Maine

Arches, Utah

Badlands, South Dakota

Big Bend, Texas

Biscayne, Florida

Bryce Canyon, Utah

Canyonlands, Utah

Capitol Reef, Utah

Carlsbad Caverns, New Mexico

Channel Islands, California

Crater Lake, Oregon

Death Valley, California

Denali, Alaska

Dry Tortugas, Florida

Everglades, Florida

Gates of the Arctic, Alaska

Glacier, British Columbia

Glacier Bay, Alaska

Grand Canyon, Arizona

Grand Teton, Wyoming

Great Basin, Nevada

Great Smoky Mountains, North Carolina and Tennessee

Guadalupe Mountains, Texas

Haleakala, Hawaii

Hawaii Volcanoes, Hawaii

Hot Springs, Arkansas

Isle Royale, Michigan

Joshua Tree, California

Katmai, Alaska

Kenai Fjords, Alaska

Kobuk Valley, Alaska

Lake Clark, Alaska

Lassen Volcanic, California

Mammoth Cave, Kentucky

Mesa Verde, Colorado

Mount Rainier, Washington

North Cascades, Washington

Olympic, Washington

Petrified Forest, Arizona

Redwood, California

Rocky Mountain, Colorado

Saguaro, Arizona

Sequoia/Kings Canyon, California

Shenandoah, Virginia

Theodore Roosevelt, North Dakota

Virgin Islands

Voyageurs, Minnesota

Wind Cave, South Dakota

Wrangell Saint Elias, Alaska

Yellowstone, Idaho, Montana, Wyoming

Yosemite, California

Zion, Utah

NATIONAL PARKS EMPLOYMENT DATA

124 North San Francisco Street, Suite 100
Flagstaff, AZ 86001
     or
P.O. Box 1392
Flagstaff, AZ 86002
(520) 779-5300
bbenton@pinecountry.net

WEB SITES

Administrative Careers with America
http://www.doi.gov/hrm/pmanager/st4k.html
Administrative Careers with America is another venue for seeking
employment with the National Park Service. This program provides
applicants with the opportunity to compete through an examination.
Park ranger positions come under Group VI, Law Enforcement
and Investigation.

EEK! Environmental Education for Kids
http://www.dnr.state.wi.us/org/caer/ce/eek/job/ranger.htm
Diary of a park ranger.

National Park Service
http://www.nps.gov
The National Park Service site has all the information you need on
    pursuing a career as a park ranger and the various duties and
    geographic locations available to you.

Natural Resources Defense Council
http://www.nrdc.org
OnEarth magazine online is a good source of information on wildlife
    preservation.

BOOKS

Burby, Liza N. *A Day in the Life of a Park Ranger*. New York, NY: The
    Rosen Publishing Group, Inc., 1999.

Burnett, Jim. *Hey Ranger!: True Tales of Humor & Misadventure
    from America's National Parks*. New York, NY: Taylor Trade
    Publishing, 2005.

Muench, David, Tom Kiernan, and Ruth Rudner. *Our National Parks*.
    Portland, OR: Graphic Arts Center Publishing Company, 2005.

National Geographic Society. *National Geographic Guide to the
    National Parks of the United States*. Fifth edition. Washington, DC:
    National Geographic, 2006.

O'Gara, Geoff. *Frommer's Yellowstone and Grand Teton National Parks*.
    New York, NY: IDG Books Worldwide, 2000.

MAGAZINES

National Parks Magazine
http://www.npca.org/magazine
The magazine of the National Parks Conservation Association.

New World Journal
330 W. 56th Street, Suite 3G
New York, NY 10019-4244
(212) 265-7970
Broad-based environmental magazine.

Summit
Summit Publications, Inc.
1221 May Street
Hood River, OR 97031
(503) 387-2200
Magazine promoting mountains, culture, environment, and adventure.

Wilderness Trails
Wilderness Trails, Inc.
712 Satori Drive
Petaluma, CA 94954
(707) 762-8839
Magazine for outdoor activists—combines outdoor adventure and
   environmental concerns.

VIDEOS/DVDS

North America's National Parks (2007)
Topics Entertainment.

8

URBAN GARDENER

If you grew up in the suburbs or the country, you may take for granted the green grass and variety of trees and flowers that are all around you. City dwellers experience less nature in their daily lives, and nowhere is this more true than in impoverished urban areas where land often becomes abandoned. Considering the wasted potential of these empty lots and the very real danger of malnutrition to which the impoverished are exposed, it quickly becomes evident that there is a clear need for community gardening.

Description

A recent survey by the National Gardening Association found that 300,000 households participated in and enjoyed the produce of a community garden. Fifty million households reported having no involvement with a community garden, but 13.5 percent of them expressed interest in becoming involved if one were nearby. This is where you come in. Why not take the initiative and help start a community garden in a vacant lot near you?

Those involved in community gardening get to combine a love for nature and knowledge of gardening and horticulture with a sense of responsibility to help others. Many nonprofit "urban greening" or community gardening projects are devoted to both restoring unused land and providing environmental education for the people who live there. When working for one of these projects, you may be required to work in youth or after-school programs that promote nutrition through cultivating healthful foods. You should be willing to pitch in and do some tough labor: cleaning and clearing vacant lots; maintaining sheds, benches, and picnic tables; composting leaves and unsalable produce; and, of course, weeding, planting, and harvesting in the gardens. As

A gardener harvests vegetables from a community garden in Seattle, Washington.

a horticulturist for one of these programs, you may be in charge of coordinating horticultural education by preparing workshops, on-site demonstrations, and training sessions. You may even spend some time staffing a garden's farmers' market, selling your produce to restaurants, to local markets, or directly to the public. And, although in the middle of a city, you could end up working in a variety of agricultural settings, such as a small farm, a garden, a greenhouse, a tree nursery, or an outdoor classroom.

Eventually, you may find yourself moving out of the garden and into a more administrative position within the project that hired you. You may wish to become involved in helping communities set up gardens, rather than setting them up with your own hands. In this capacity, you will recruit, instruct, and support volunteer leaders as they create and maintain productive community gardens. You will provide advice on starting a neighborhood garden project over the phone or through newsletters or a Web site; relay accurate information on food growing and preservation; put neighborhood gardeners in touch with local gardening resources; distribute donated seeds, plants, and gardening supplies and tools; and seek funding or sponsorship from sources both private (companies and individuals) and public (local, state, and/or federal governments). While many of the people who head these groups have higher degrees in education, horticulture, or community development, extensive hands-on experience will allow you to make contacts with these groups and pursue any opportunities that arise. Community college courses or training programs in education, community development, or horticulture/agriculture would be a plus. Since these gardening groups are nonprofit, you will not earn very much money. The real reward of this work is seeing a neighborhood transformed, both physically and emotionally.

The Goals of a Community Garden

- Increase residents' access to fresh and nutritious fruits and vegetables
- Decrease families' grocery bills
- Beautify the neighborhood and create a safe, communal gathering place
- Foster youth and community leadership and organizational skills
- Foster entrepreneurial skills and forge business-community ties by marketing and selling surplus produce

Volunteer students participate in the Project 2000 barrio clean-up and beautification effort in Austin, Texas.

- Provide young people who are interested in agricultural or horticultural careers with valuable work experience
- Provide young people with a positive, productive, after-school activity
- Build strong community ties and increase social interaction and civic participation
- Encourage neighborhood self-reliance
- Increase self-esteem, self-confidence, and education of young people
- Promote healthier communities

Training/Education

Get out there and dig! Any relevant experience you can get by working at a nursery or in a greenhouse will help you pursue this career.

The ability to work well with others in a learning environment is also essential. While some programs may seek those with degrees in education, relevant experience and dedication is usually a good substitute. You should start getting practice in this area through community service, youth development, summer camps, or youth ministry programs. Communication skills are also very important.

Volunteer or try to get a paid internship with an established urban greening program. Once you have your foot in the door and prove to your supervisors that you are a hard worker and a good organizer, keep an eye out for paying jobs that may open up.

Bearing Fruit

The United States Department of Agriculture estimates that urban gardeners involved in its programs grow about $16 million worth of fresh food annually.

A survey by the Rutgers Cooperative Extension found that 13 percent of respondents felt that a community garden had improved their neighborhood by cleaning blighted areas and increasing neighborliness.

Ninety-five percent of employees and patients participating in a Center for Health Design study of hospital gardens claimed that gardening had therapeutic benefits, such as making the gardeners feel more productive and healthy, less stressed, and more able to tolerate treatment and medicine.

The Greening of North America
(For more success stories, visit www.cityfarmer.org.)

- Puerto Rican community gardeners in New York cultivate vegetables, fruit, and medicinal and culinary herbs. They also construct one- and two-room wood frame structures known as *casitas,* or "little houses."

- Lettuce Link improves the nutritional opportunities of low-income people in Seattle through garden development in low-income communities, basic garden education, seed and plant distribution at food banks, and coordination of produce donations.

- In 2000, volunteer garden leaders in Cleveland coordinated the planting of 206 community gardens covering 33 acres of previously vacant land. Over 80 percent of the gardens are found in Cleveland's poorest neighborhoods.

- Vacant lots are a common sight in big urban areas. In Philadelphia, one of the largest comprehensive urban greening programs in North America is working to turn these blights into a source of pride and sustenance. The Philadelphia Urban Gardening Project reports that community gardeners eat produce

(continued)

from their gardens five months of the year, food is shared with neighbors and relatives on a weekly basis, and 40 percent of the gardeners share food with church or community organizations.

FOR MORE INFORMATION

ASSOCIATIONS

Cities Feeding People
http://www.cityfarmer.org/IDRCbrochure.html
For more information about Cities Feeding People, contact Brenda-Lee Wilson at blwilson@idrc.ca.

Eco-Village, Los Angeles
3551 White House Place
Los Angeles, CA 90004
(213) 738-1254
crsp@igc.apc.org
http://www.laecovillage.org

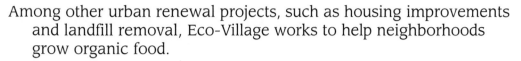

Among other urban renewal projects, such as housing improvements and landfill removal, Eco-Village works to help neighborhoods grow organic food.

Community Food Security Coalition
P.O. Box 209
Venice, CA 90294
(310) 822-5410
http://www.foodsecurity.org
The Community Food Security Coalition publishes a newsletter on how to start a community garden.

Keep America Beautiful
9 West Broad Street
Stamford, CT 06902
(203) 323-8987
http://www.kab.org

Urban Ecology
http://www.urbanecology.org
Founded in 1975, Urban Ecology assists communities in changing their land use and building patterns. Take a look at the excellent quarterly magazine for an idea of what is going on in our nation's cities, and how you can help create change.

TRAINING PROGRAMS
Alternative Farming Systems Information Center
National Agriculture Library, Room 304
10301 Baltimore Avenue
Beltsville, MD 20705-2351
(301) 504-6559
afsic@nal.usda.gov

WEB SITES
American Community Gardening Association
http://www.communitygarden.org

America the Beautiful Fund
http://america-the-beautiful.org

City Farmer's Urban Agriculture Notes
http://www.cityfarmer.org

EcoNet
http://www.igc.org

Jobs in Urban Agriculture
http://www.cityfarmer.org/jobs.html

KidsGardening!
http://www.kidsgardening.com/grants.asp

National Gardening
http://www.garden.org

Southern California Non-profit Organizations Working for Sustainability
http://www.scced.org/sust_orgs/parkorg.html
Listing of parks, urban farming, and urban forests associations in
California.

BOOKS

Bell, Dale, and Harry Wiland. *Edens Lost & Found: How Ordinary Citizens Are Restoring Our Great American Cities*. White River Jct., VT: Chelsea Green Publishing, 2006.

Blanc, Patrick. *The Vertical Garden: From Nature to the City*. New York, NY: W. W. Norton, 2008.

Dunnett, Nigel, and Noel Kingsbury. *Planting Green Roofs and Living Walls*. Portland, OR: Timber Press, 2008.

Feldt, Barbara. *Garden Your City*. New York, NY: Taylor Trade Publishing, 2005.

Forman, Richard T. T. *Urban Regions: Ecology and Planning Beyond the City*. Cambridge, MA: Cambridge University Press, 2008

Henderson, Elizabeth, and Robyn Van En. *Sharing the Harvest: A Citizens Guide to Community Supported Agriculture.* Revised and expanded edition. White River Junction, VT: Chelsea Green Publishing, 2007.

Lawson, Laura J. *City Bountiful: A Century of Community Gardening in America.* Berkeley, CA: University of California Press, 2005.

NEWSLETTERS

Urban Agriculture Notes
Canada's Office of Urban Agriculture
Vancouver, BC
cityfarm@interchange.ubc.ca
http://www.cityfarmer.org

MULTIMEDIA

City Farmer TV, a video podcast of the Vancouver community gardens.
http://web.mac.com/cityfarmer/CityFarmerTV/VideoPodcast/
VideoPodcast.html

Marketplace for the Mind: An Agricultural Education Resource
http://www.marketplaceforthemind.state.pa.us/m4m/lib/m4m/
homepage.asp

9

WHALE WATCHER

Can you imagine yourself aboard a ship, sailing the seven seas while peacefully pursuing whales in their natural habitat and guiding passengers on a nautical adventure they will never forget? Whale-watching crews provide an important service to the public, help raise money for nature conservation, and enjoy one of the most awe-inspiring careers available.

Description

Whale watching, as a commercial activity, began in 1955 in North America along the Southern California coast. Today, whale-watching tours sail the oceans and bays of some seventy countries and represent one of the fastest growing of all global tourism sectors. The Whale and Dolphin Conservation Society (WDCS) specifies that a safe whale-watch boat features an experienced skipper and a crew who are well trained in first aid and rescue skills. As a member of the crew, you are responsible for educating the passengers on board about the whales and other marine life observed on your outing. Many whale-watching operations invite research scientists on board, so you may also be involved in research projects with the naturalists who form part of your group.

According to the WDCS, a good guide will demonstrate several valuable characteristics. She or he should be lively and entertaining, knowledgeable about all local marine life, and able to interpret the behavior of whales spotted on the outing, including the whales' singing and mating practices. A guide should also encourage guests to become interested in conservation and point them to further sources of information on whales, such as nearby museums, bookstores, and science centers. Above all, whale-watching guides should care about both the whales and their guests. The welfare of the whales should be the top priority; a whale

The skeletons of a humpback whale and a blue whale hang from the ceiling of the Whaling Museum in New Bedford, Massachusetts.

should never be disturbed or endangered in order to give guests a closer view or bigger thrill, nor should the lives of passengers be threatened by reckless behavior.

Education/Training

Learning by doing is the key here, but you may need to do a little digging to find an operation with enough resources to offer you a valuable internship. The Isle of Shoals, northern New England's oldest whale-watching company, promotes an internship program that teaches students of all ages and

Whale watchers get a close look at a gray whale in the San Ignacio Lagoon in Baja, California.

backgrounds about sea life and how it fits into the larger ecological picture. Interns in this program act as apprentices to more experienced guides and then lead small tour groups themselves. This type of experience is a wonderful opportunity to learn all about field identification of various species, practice research and observation methods, and gain marine navigation and communication skills. Best of all, you don't need any background to be successful; the Isle of Shoals program and others like it will give you all the training you need.

The History of Whale Watching

Today, commercial whale watching is a billion-dollar industry conducted in seventy different countries and territories, yet the industry has very humble origins. In 1955, a San Diego fisherman, Chuck Chamberlin, organized the first commercial whale-watching trip, charging customers one dollar to climb on his boat and cruise the waters of Southern California looking for gray whales. This idea began to catch on, other fishermen began taking customers out to sea, and soon many people were traveling to the West Coast just to embark on whale-watching adventures.

By the 1970s, whale-watching tours became available on the East Coast, and in 1980 a Spanish fisherman began offering similar expeditions in Gibraltar Bay. Before long, whale-watching tours were also being offered in the Caribbean, South America, Australia, New Zealand, and Japan. What began as one fisherman's attempt to make a little extra money has become a huge industry. Many people, from fishermen to Wall Street traders, have followed Chamberlin's lead and left behind more traditional careers in order to establish whale-watching tours from the Arctic to the South Pacific.

Outlook

Since 1955, when Chuck Chamberlin led the very first commercial whale-watching trip in his fishing boat, the industry has continued to expand and shows no sign of stopping. With ecotourism in general becoming more and more popular, whale-watching employment prospects seem very bright. Just be sure that you choose a reputable operator that will not take advantage of you, harm or endanger the whales, or put the safety of its guests at risk. You will not get rich as a whale-watching guide; you will most likely draw a modest salary or hourly wage, and some operators encourage tipping. If you save your money, you may someday be able to buy your own boat or fleet of boats and launch your own whale-watching operation.

Fun Facts About Whales

- Most large whales travel in small schools (called pods), but some swim in pairs or even alone. Whales are most often observed in open ocean during their migration from feeding to breeding grounds, a voyage of several thousands of miles.

- Watching whales as they migrate is a fascinating experience. Each winter, California gray whales travel down the Pacific coast from their summer feeding grounds in the Bering Sea and Arctic Ocean to Mexico's Baja Peninsula, where they breed and give birth. It is the longest mammal migration on Earth—12,000 miles round trip each year!

- On your whale watches, you may observe the whales eating. A blue whale eats a lot of krill, or plankton—up to the equivalent of a fully grown African elephant every day.

FOR MORE INFORMATION

WHALE WATCHING LOCATION DIRECTORY

Whales can be spotted in their natural habitats all around the world. Can you blame the whales for choosing these beautiful, often awe-inspiring places to live?

Andenes, Norway

Antarctica

Argentina

Baja California, Mexico

Brazil

British Virgin Islands

Churchill, Manitoba

Colombia

Dominican Republic

Ecuador

Hawaii

Lambert's Bay, South Africa

Monkey Mia, Western Australia

Moray Firth, Scotland

New Zealand

Ogasawara Islands, Japan

Península Valdés, Patagonia, Argentina

St. Lawrence River and the Gulf of St. Lawrence, Quebec

San Juan Islands

Tañon Strait, the Philippines

Washington State

WEB SITES

Gorp.com
http://www.gorp.com/gorp/interact/guests/ellis.htm
A forum of whale questions answered by expert Richard Ellis.

Greenpeace Global Whale Sanctuary
http://www.greenpeace.org/international/campaigns/oceans/whaling

Greenpeace International
http://www.greenpeace.org

Ocean Alliance
http://www.whale.org

Organisation Cetacea (ORCA)
http://www.orcaweb.org.uk
ORCA is a whale and dolphin society established to promote enjoyment
of cetaceans and participation in whale and dolphin research.

WDCS Whale Adoption Project
http://www.whales.org/news/dolphinSMART1-07.asp

The Whale & Dolphin Adoption Project
http://www.adopt-a-dolphin.com

The Whale & Dolphin Adoption Project
http://www.adopt-a-dolphin.com

Whales-online
http://www.whales-online.org
By becoming a member of the Sea Station Network, you receive
regular updates about whale campaigns and news items from
around the world.

Whales on the Net—A Whale-Watching Directory
http://www.whales.org.au/watch/index.html

Whale Watching Alaska
http://www.alaskawhalewatching.com

Whale Watching Spoken Here
http://whalespoken.org

BOOKS

Chadwick, Douglas H. *The Grandest of Lives: Eye to Eye with Whales.*
New York, NY: Sierra Club, 2008.

Fromm, Peter. *Whale Tales: Human Interactions with Whales*. Friday Harbor, WA: Whale Tales Press, 2000.

Jones, David. *Whales*. Toronto, Canada: Whitecap Books, 2005.

Rylant, Cynthia. *The Whales*. New York, NY: Blue Sky Press, 2000.

VIDEOS/DVDS

Awesome Whales for Kids (2006)
The Whale Video Company.

Humans of the Sea: Killer Whales and the People Who Watch Them (2007)
Video Age Productions.

What to Do About Whales? (2007)
Second Nature Films.

10

RIVER GUIDE

If you love adventure as much as you love being outdoors, a career as a river guide could be perfect for you. Whitewater rafting guides are truly independent spirits who lead tours on rivers throughout the world. Because of their valuable skills, it is not necessary for them to commit to any one company. River guides can find work wherever the current takes them!

106

Description

Picture it: You're battling against a river, wild with twists and turns and unpredictable rapids. Actually, it is more like you are one with the river; a seasoned guide learns to read and understand the water. Since white-water guides teach their skills to beginners, they get to earn a living completely outdoors. They are experts in all areas of outdoor living and emergency survival, and, of course, they can safely manage a boat on swift water. As a guide, you must teach your team the basics of safety and rafting technique and be prepared for unexpected emergencies on the river.

Training

The most common way of learning how to be a guide is by attending a river guide school. The three- to seven-day training sessions are run by many different companies (usually outdoors outfitters) and cost several hundred dollars. Ken Streater, president of the white-water rafting tour company Wilderness Trips, says that these schools are the most cost-effective training option. While you may find an outfitter who is willing to hire you as a river guide without formal training, your new boss may take advantage of your inexperience and your eagerness and he or she may not pay you fairly. In any case, an outfitter who hires inexperienced guides is not reputable and will probably endanger his or

A group goes white-water rafting on the Salmon River in Idaho.

her staff and customers with shoddy equipment and negligent practices.

The best route to landing a good guide job, then, is to sign up for a rafting course. It is a relatively small investment and an awful lot of fun. Gaining this formal experience will increase your chances of getting hired by one of the better outfitters, from whom you will learn good business and rafting practices. This in turn may allow you to start your own river tour company someday. As Ken Streater

says, "It's better to start earning money in your own right than to be stuck in a corporation mentality."

The river guide school you choose should be staffed by experienced, knowledgeable teachers and mentors. They should have decades of experience leading trips and teaching students. Every aspect of guiding a raft down river should be taught, from "reading" white water (predicting its flow and strength based on its surface appearance), maneuvering boats, and knot tying, to safe food preparation, composting, and recycling. The cost of a six- to eight-day course can range from about $500 to $1,000. A workshop on swift water emergency and rescue techniques should be included in your course. In this section, you will unwrap rafts, perform flipped-raft drills, use flip lines (to right an upended raft) and throw bags (for flotation), swim in rapids, swim in and out of eddies, practice foot-entrapment exercises and linecrossing of rapids, learn about hypothermia prevention and treatment, and study the other skills needed to manage a white-water emergency. Generally, students must supply some of their own gear, such as a tent, a sleeping bag, a sleeping pad, wet and dry suits, river shoes, and outdoor clothing.

A good river school will maintain a high instructor-to-student ratio (such as one to four or five) in order to ensure individual attention. Carefully supervised solo river sessions

A team of rescue workers prepare to search for missing people in the Saxeten brook near Interlaken, Switzerland.

should be coupled with more hands-on instruction; this allows students to put theory into practice and discover solutions to problems on their own, thereby giving them the confidence they will need to lead their own expeditions later on. Some schools recommend that students take a course in first aid and CPR (check with the local American Red Cross to find classes) and read about river running before enrolling in a training program. The Whitewater Voyages Guide School also recommends that potential guides spend

A River Guide's Safety Code

As a river guide, you will have to observe certain safety codes for white-water rafting. Here are some of the guidelines:

- Make sure you and your party are all competent swimmers.
- Be sure everyone is wearing a life preserver, shoulder protection, and a correctly fitted helmet.
- Do not enter a rapid unless you are reasonably sure that you can get through it without injury or mishap.
- Make sure that each boat contains at least three people and that a party contains no less than two boats. Never boat alone.
- Have a realistic sense of your skills and the ability of your guests (taking into account their fitness, age, anxiety levels, and health). Do not attempt to navigate rapids that are beyond your party's abilities.
- Be knowledgeable in rescue and self-rescue skills, CPR, and first aid. Carry the equipment necessary for unexpected emergencies, such as knives, whistles,

(continued)

flashlights, folding saws, guidebooks, maps, food, waterproof matches, extra clothing, and repair kits.

- Be sure that your boat and gear are all in good working order. Test any new equipment before you take a party downriver.
- Never lead a party under the influence of drugs or alcohol and do not allow members of your party to partake in either. Drugs and alcohol use can dull reflexes and impair a person's decision-making ability, thus leading to potentially serious accidents.

a day playing around in an oar boat on a lake—practicing sitting, holding the oars, and being comfortable in the boat—before taking on any rapids.

Outlook

"One of the nice things about guiding now is that the world has gotten so much smaller in the last decade," says Ken Streater. "Adventure trips take place all around the world all during the year. Plenty of people work year-round just as guides and earn a successful living while doing what they love." On average, a river guide can make from $65 to $110 for a one-day trip. Average starting wages are $8 to $10 an hour, plus bonuses.

Profile

Ken Streater, president, Wilderness Trips

"I went rafting once with my dad and it bit me hard!" Ken Streater says of his offbeat career choice. Originally from California, he took his first trip in the Sierra Nevada. He has since traveled all over the world, re-creating the thrilling experience of taming a wild river. Ken got into the field the most common way—by going to a weeklong river guide school. "That school was the foundation for my career. It gave me all the necessary skills."

Before he started rafting, Ken worked as an assistant manager at a sporting goods store. This experience was a crash course in personnel issues (hiring the right people, firing the wrong people, forming a cooperative and productive team), which served him well when he started his own outfitting companies, first in Alaska, then in the Pacific Northwest, where he now resides. Ken has also run tours in Scandinavia and was a guide on the first joint Soviet-American river trip in Siberia.

His advice for river-reading enthusiasts? "The best thing you can do is go on one of these trips! It will give you a feel for whether it's something you can see yourself doing."

FOR MORE INFORMATION

GUIDE SCHOOLS

Arkansas River Tours Whitewater Guide Training
http://www.arkansasrivertours.com/guide-t.htm
ART guides are trained to teach paddling techniques, river
characteristics, local history, and the riparian environment. Call
(800) 321-4352 for an application.

Destination Wilderness
http://www.wildernesstrips.com
This is Ken Streater's company, which specializes in wilderness rafting,
kayaking, trekking, culture, and wildlife journeys in the most
incredible places on Earth.

Whitewater Voyages Guide School
http://www.whitewatervoyages.com/schools/wwschools.html
Intensive workshops and instruction in guiding oar and paddle rafts,
encompassing fundamental skills of reading white water and
maneuvering boats.

WEB SITES

E-Raft.com
http://www.e-raft.com/default.htm
E-Raft is an excellent, comprehensive online resource for white-water
rafting throughout North America.

GORP.com
http://www.gorp.com/gorp/activity/paddling/pad_guid.htm

Just name your destination: GORP.com has a map of the world that features all the best rivers you can take on.

Riversearch.com
http://www.riversearch.com
Excellent blog of the top sites for white-water trips and companies all over the world.

BOOKS

Jennings, Gayle. *Water-Based Tourism, Sport, Leisure, and Recreation Experiences*. Burlington, MA: Butterworth-Heinemann, 2006.

McGinnis, William. *The Guide's Guide Augmented: Reflections on Guiding Professional River Trips*. Hong Kong: Whitewater Voyages, 2005.

McGuffin, Gary, and Joanie McGuffin. *Paddle Your Own Kayak: An Illustrated Guide to the Art of Kayaking*. Ontario, Canada: Boston Mills Press, 2008.

Nealy, William. *Kayak: The New Frontier: The Animated Manual of Intermediate and Advanced Whitewater Technique*. Birmingham, AL: Menasha Ridge Press, 2007.

Watson, Tom. *Kids Gone Paddlin': The Young Paddler's Guide to Having More Fun Outdoors*. Minneapolis, MN: Creative Publishing International, 2008.

MAGAZINES

Che-Mun
The Journal of Canadian Wilderness Canoeing
Box 548, Station O
Toronto, ON M4A 2P1
Canada
(416) 789-2142
mpeake@inforamp.net
http://www.canoe.ca/che-mun/home.html

Kayak Magazine
309 Edgeway Loop
Fayetteville, NC 28314
http://www.kayakmagazine.com

Paddler
The Paddling Group Inc.
P.O. Box 1341
Eagle, ID 83616
(208) 939-4500
http://www.paddlermagazine.com

Rapid—**Canada's Whitewater Magazine**
http://www.rapidmag.com

ARTICLES

"Paddling Skills and How to Battle the Rapids."
http://www.gorp.com/gorp/activity/paddling/pad_how.htm
A huge selection of tips on battling the rapids.

Cleveland, Paul. "Ready to Raft."
http://www.gorp.com/gorp/gear/features/raftwear.htm
Tips on how to dress for your white-water adventure.

11

WILDLAND FIRE MANAGER

Managing wildland fires is one of the most physically demanding jobs you can have! It is also dirty and grueling (try eighteen or twenty hours a day for as long as six months on end). This career is not for everyone. But if you love being in the woods and are hardworking, brave, and respectful of nature's awe-inspiring beauty and power, you may have what it takes to be a wildland firefighter.

Fire spotters scan forests for outbreaks of fire from observation towers like this one.

Description

Woodland firefighters tackle the huge, powerful flames that can engulf hundreds of acres of forest land in a matter of hours. There are a number of positions within the category of wildland firefighting, such as fire spotters (firefighters posted in lookout towers), smoke jumpers, and hotshots. Professionals, like timber managers and biologists, round out the team. The positions all share some common requirements, including the ability to hike across long distances carrying at least forty-five pounds on your back. You may

Hotshots

Hotshots, an elite, highly trained crew of firefighters with the U.S. Forest Service, work in crews of twenty highly trained men and women who live together and are often called upon to travel wherever they are needed. Their specialty is situations where wildfires begin to threaten urban and suburban areas. According to the National Park Service, hotshots are generally given assignments on the toughest part of a fire.

have to follow fires in some very remote places for weeks on end.

Education/Training

You must be knowledgeable in basic first aid and CPR before you even inquire about one of these high-risk positions.

Entry-level positions can be difficult to snare in this field. One method is to start out as a forestry aide or technician; consider these lower-rung positions as a kind of internship. These jobs can consist of backbreaking work but are an excellent apprenticeship to the world of wildland firefighting and may even open the door to timber, recreation, range, fisheries, wildlife, or surveying positions with the National

Fighting Fires from the Sky

Smoke jumpers are firefighters who parachute into burning forests in order to fight blazes. They are flown into the remote areas that hotshot crews and other firefighters cannot reach. They jump in groups of two to ten people, with each person carrying 100 pounds of equipment on his or her back, and they fight the fire for three to five days. When finished, they gather up their equipment and hike to the nearest access road, which is often many miles away. Smoke jumpers are drawn

Smoke jumpers stand by the edge of the firebreak and put out new fires that flare up.

from the ranks of experienced firefighters from the Forest Service, Bureau of Land Management, or state forest fire departments. They often also have experience as farmers, park rangers, or ranchers. Would-be smoke jumpers must be physically fit and must successfully complete a boot camp–style training session. Smoke jumpers say the pay is good, but it is the scenery, adventure, and strong sense of camaraderie that keeps them coming back year after year.

Park Service. Firefighters who are employed by the state and national parks are not required to have college degrees, but a high school diploma is a prerequisite. And each progressive level of the job requires additional work-related training. Below are two of the academies that offer such hands-on coursework:

Colorado Wildfire Academy
http://www.cowildfireacademy.com

National Interagency Fire Center—National Course Development (NIFC)
http://www.nifc.gov

Outlook

Federal and state fire management agencies often need temporary firefighters, so seasonal work is a good way to get your foot in the door. The personnel office of a forest supervisor lets the state employment office do its recruiting, so inquire there first. State offices begin accepting federal applications in February. If the state office refers you to the forest supervisor, you will then be considered for employment on a crew. Fire managers start at about $9 per hour, with experienced veterans earning as much as $16 an hour. A top salary would be about $25,000 for a six-month stint.

Firestarters

You may be interested to learn that wildland firefighters sometimes must start fires as well as put them out.

Fires are a natural and necessary element in nature. In fact, a forest's health requires the occasional fire. A fire can clear away old, dead growth and make room for younger, more healthy trees. The ash that results from a fire is rich in nutrients and acts as a natural fertilizer. However, for a good part of this century, government policy mandated that fires not be allowed to burn. According to the National Park Service, more than 100 years of fighting wildfires has altered the landscape. This has resulted in important changes to the forest environment, such as a heavy buildup of dead vegetation, dense stands of trees, a shift to species that have not evolved and adapted to fire, and, occasionally, even an increase in non-native fire-prone plants. Because of these conditions, today's fires tend to be larger, burn hotter, and spread farther and faster, making them more severe, more dangerous, and more costly in human, economic, and ecological terms. In recent years, during droughts in California, Washington, and Florida, we have seen how easily fires can start and how quickly they rage out of control when a forest is filled with too much growth and brush. As a result, controlled burns are now part of national forest policy.

Land managers must balance wildland fire suppression with the beneficial use of fire for resource management. A prescribed fire is any fire intentionally ignited to reduce flammable fuels, such as the accumulation of brush and logs on forest floors, or to help restore ecosystem health.

FOR MORE INFORMATION

ASSOCIATIONS

International Association of Fire Fighters
http://www.iaff.org

WEB SITES

California Professional Firefighters
http://www.cpf.org/go/cpf

Colorado Wildfire Academy
http://www.cowildfireacademy.com

Fire Careers/Training with the National Park Service
http://www.nps.gov/fire/employment/employment.cfm

The Firefighters Bookstore
http://www.firebooks.com

National Firefighting Hall of Heroes
http://www.hallofflame.org/hallhero.htm

Wildfire News
http://www.wildfirenews.com

Wild Fire News Archive
Women Firefighters Resource Page
http://www.i-women.org

BOOKS

Beil, Karen Magnuson. *Fire in Their Eyes: Wildfires and the People Who Fight Them*. New York, NY: Harcourt Brace, 1999.

Fritz, Richard A. *Tools of the Trade: Firefighting Hand Tools and Their Use*. Saddle Brook, NJ: Fire Engineering Books and Videos, 1997.

Lowe, Joseph D., Jeanne Mesick, Kasey Young, and Mark Huth. *Wildland Firefighting Practices*. Florence, KY: Delmar Publishers, 2000.

Maclean, John N. *Fire and Ashes: On the Front Lines Battling Wildfires*. New York, NY: Holt Paperbacks, 2004.

Desmond, Matthew. *On the Fireline: Living and Dying with Wildland Firefighters*. Chicago, IL: University Of Chicago Press, 2007.

Gigliotti, Jim. *Smoke Jumpers*. New York, NY: Child's World, 2006.

Holdcroft, Gary Phillip. *Walking Through The Ashes: A Volunteer Firefighter's Perspective on the Rodeo-Chediski Fire*. Victoria, BC, Canada: Trafford Publishing, 2006.

Pyne, Stephen. *Tending Fire: Coping with America's Wildland Fires*. Washington, DC: Island Press, 2004.

Pyne, Stephen J. *Fire in America: A Cultural History of Wildland and Rural Fire*. Seattle, WA: University of Washington Press, 1997.

MAGAZINES

Firehouse
http://www.firehouse.com

Fire Nuggets
http://www.firenuggets.com

Wildland Firefighter
http://www.fire-police-ems.com/books/95030.htm

VIDEOS/DVDS

California Firestorm 2007, Volume 1 (2008)
Alan Simmons Productions.

Emergency in the Streets, Vol. 6 Special Edition: Brush Fire! (2005)
Valley News Inc.

Wildfire (1994)
Audubon Video.

Wildfires: Fighting Fire with Fire (1995)
A&E.

Wildland Essentials—Fighting Fire in the Interface (1996)
Wildland Fire Consultants and Seminars.

12

NATURE PHOTOGRAPHER

Starting out as a nature photographer, all you need is a camera (and it need not be an expensive one), patience, and an artistic eye. Why patience? In the wild, a lot of animals are shy and timid, especially when humans are nearby. Get ready to spend a lot of time outdoors—in the woods, deep in a swamp, on the peak of a mountain, or on the side of a volcano. The really good news is that first those spots are your classroom, and then they are your office. Nice work if you can get it!

Description

The range of career possibilities for a nature photographer is very wide. While not everyone can land a job with *National Geographic* or *Nature* magazine, there are plenty of opportunities for photographers who want to focus their lenses on the natural world. Photographers can earn a living by getting a full-time position at a magazine or other publication, but most nature photographers work on a freelance basis. Freelance work is less steady, but it is a good option for photographers who have built up a reputation or an address book full of clients. Keep your eyes open for opportunities, as they can come from unexpected sources. Businesses, such as outdoor sporting goods and gardening companies, need professional-quality photographers to illustrate their promotional materials (catalogs, Web sites, posters, and other display materials). The greeting card and calendar industries are also possible venues for your images.

Simply stated, a nature photographer must have a love of and respectful appreciation for nature. It is also very important to have a good eye, a visual instinct that allows you to hunt out the most interesting subjects and frame them in the most compelling way. Beyond these essential

A nature photographer takes shots of Monument Valley in Arizona.

attributes, the technical aspects of photography can be learned through a combination of formal study (in high school, community college classes, or YMCA workshops) and trial and error.

Nature photography also involves a lot of patience, determination, and an adventurous spirit. You may have to wait for hours for the clouds to clear, for the sun to reach just the right part of the sky, or for an animal to pass before your lens. Sometimes the light will be too harsh or too subdued; sometimes animals will be partly hidden by trees or grasses or will not stay still for your camera. You will have to learn how to cope with these frustrations and how to compensate for potential limitations. Sometimes only one shot from dozens of pictures will be worthwhile; you must not let frustration and disappointment prevent you from trying again the next day. Nature photographers must also be adventurous and willing to go to remote and inhospitable places, where the weather may be harsh, in order to take great pictures.

The Nature Photographer's Code of Ethics

- Humans should appear in nature photographs only when they enhance a picture's narrative.
- Pictures of cultivated plants, still-life arrangements, domestic animals, or stuffed and mounted animals are not considered examples of nature photography.
- Photographs manipulated in any way (by computers or airbrushing, for example) are not considered to be true nature photography.
- Do not disturb wild creatures by playing loud music, littering, driving recklessly, or driving off approved roads. If an animal seems agitated, draw back.

- Learn about the behavior of your animal subjects before photographing them. Know when not to interfere with animals' life cycles and respect their routines. Do not approach nests or dens too closely. Never remove fledglings from their nests.

- It is acceptable to remove insects and reptiles from their habitat for photographing, as long as they are returned. Permission to do so from the proper authorities must be granted.

- It is never acceptable to anesthetize an animal for the purposes of nature photography.

- Nocturnal creatures should be photographed in the early morning or late afternoon when they are less active. This will make it easier for you to get the shot, but you will not be disrupting them.

- Cave formations and paintings should never be removed, broken, or tampered with in any way.

- Avoid trampling on grasslands, marshes, and wild-flower patches when photographing plants and flowers. Damage to these plants and flowers affects all species in the ecosystem. Stay on designated trails. Wildflowers should never be picked.

Education/Training

Professional nature photographer Ruth Hoyt recommends taking a class, even a general adult education course, as a start. "You can learn on your own, but it's good to get going with some instruction for the technical aspects. Although sometimes it's better to make mistakes and find out later why."

The North American Nature Photography Association sponsors a student scholarship program that is a young photographer's dream come true. Ten high school students are selected annually to attend workshops and trade shows as well as two preliminary days of instructional classes and photo opportunities. Hoyt started participating in the program years ago when she was an aspiring photographer. She says that every year the students put together such a beautiful show that it is just as rewarding for her as it is for them. To be accepted, Hoyt says all you need to demonstrate are a love of nature and a keen interest in nature photography.

Outlook

To get started in your new career, spend as much time as possible researching the location and species of everything you photograph. Assign yourself projects, and make every picture a learning opportunity. Hoyt says developing your writing skills can definitely set you apart from the pack.

When you feel confident in your skills, go ahead and buy a nature magazine you like and study it, and write to the photo editor for submission guidelines. The rest is up to you. Freelance earnings vary widely, depending on your reputation and experience. Full-time magazine photographers start at about $500 a week and can earn up to $60,000 or more a year (with travel expenses paid) once well established and highly regarded.

Profile

Ruth Hoyt, professional photographer

Ruth Hoyt is an accomplished nature photographer. Her favorite kind of work is shooting close-ups of small details in nature: bugs on leaves, little animals hiding in trees, small birds gliding along the water.

She fell into her career quite by accident. In 1989, her house was broken into and she found herself replacing an expensive camera she had never learned how to use. She signed herself up for a camera class at a local community center and soon discovered a talent she did not know she had. Hoyt spent that first summer with a photography group going on field trips. When she entered her first competition the following fall, her photo of a cheetah cub in a hollowed-out log won first place. She had photography fever, and snapping pictures of natural settings became her first love.

It was not long before she decided to quit her day job and devote herself full-time to nature photography. That risky move eventually paid off monetarily and in many other more important ways. Her work has appeared in National Geographic *publications, a Sierra Club book called* Mother Earth, Missouri Magazine *of the Columbia Journalism School, and dozens of other publications. Her van has over 300,000 miles on it, which should give you an idea of where her "office" is located. Currently, Hoyt directs the Valley Land Fund Wildlife Photo Contest, which entails organizing and conducting the contest, judging the entries, and compiling and publishing the book of winning photos. There is no question that she has followed her heart, and it in turn has rewarded her with this fulfilling career.*

Nature photographers work tirelessly to capture beautiful images such as this.

FOR MORE INFORMATION

ASSOCIATIONS

North American Nature Photography Association
http://www.nanpa.org

Photographic Society of America
http://www.psaphoto.org

WORKSHOPS

Apogee Photo
http://www.apogeephoto.com/photography_workshops.shtml

The Nature Workshops
http://www.natureworkshops.com

Online Photography Seminar
http://www.photo-seminars.com/index.htm

DISCUSSION GROUP

The Nature.Net Forums
http://www.nature.net/forums

WEB SITES

ENature.com
http://www.enature.com/guides/select_group.asp
Lets you identify and get information on thousands of birds and animals.

NaturePhotographers.Net Online Magazine
http://www.naturephotographers.net

Valley Land Fund Contest
http://www.valleylandfund.com

MAGAZINES

Apogee Photo
http://www.apogeephoto.com
Online photography magazine that often features the special needs of
   nature photographers.

Nature Photographer
P.O. Box 690518
Quincy, MA 02269
(617) 847-0091
http://www.naturephotographermag.com

Pop Photo.com
http://www.popphoto.com
The online home of *Popular Photography & Imaging* and
   American Photo.

BOOKS

Fitzharris, Tim. *National Audubon Society Guide to Landscape
      Photography*. Buffalo, New York, NY: Firefly Books, 2007.
Holmes, Judy. *Professional Secrets of Nature Photography: Essential Skills
      for Photographing Outdoors*. Buffalo, NY: Amherst Media, 2000.
LaPlant, Ralph, and Amy Sharpe. *Outdoor and Survival Skills for Nature
      Photographers*. Buffalo, NY: Amherst Media, 2000.
Martin, James. *Digital Photography Outdoors: A Field Guide for
      Travel and Adventure Photographers*. Seattle, WA: Mountaineers
      Books, 2008.
Sammon, Rick. *Rick Sammon's Travel and Nature Photography*. New
      York, NY: W. W. Norton, 2006.

Shaw, John. *John Shaw's Nature Photography Field Guide*. New York, NY: Watson-Guptill Publications, 2000.

Zuckerman, Jim. *Capturing Drama of Nature Photography*. Cincinnati, OH: Writers Digest Books, 2000.

GLOSSARY

blight Something that has become run down and abandoned, such as a city building, a lot, or an entire block.

boatswain Supervisor of a boat's deckhands who is also responsible for repairing fishing gear, boat equipment, and nets.

dude ranch Working horse and/or cattle ranch that is open to visitors who participate in the daily activities of the ranch.

ecology Study of the interaction between living things and their environment.

ecotourism Trips to exotic, remote, or unspoiled locations not often visited by tourists. These tours do not damage delicate ecosystems. They often benefit local economies while promoting environmental preservation and ecological sensitivity.

fire spotters Rangers posted in lookout towers who alert firefighters when a forest fire breaks out.

horticulture The science and art of growing fruits, vegetables, flowers, or plants.

hotshots Elite crew of U.S. Forest Service firefighters who specialize in forest fires that threaten urban and suburban communities.

internship Program that allows someone to receive supervised practical experience in a field of work.

nursery Establishment that grows the plants, flowers, shrubs, and trees that landscapers and groundskeepers will eventually plant in parks, gardens, golf courses, and lawns.

outfitter Company that offers tour packages, such as white-water rafting excursions.

pruning Trimming a tree's branches to control its growth and shape, and to prevent pest infestations.

seedling Young tree that is only about a foot tall.

smoke jumpers People who parachute into remote forest fires that other firefighters cannot reach.

wrangler Another word for a ranch hand. A wrangler tends to livestock, including assisting in feeding, grooming, branding, shearing, roping, herding, and birthing of the ranch animals. Wranglers also construct, repair, and clean fences, ranch buildings, and equipment.

INDEX

C

Christmas tree farmer, 9–19
   education/training needed, 13–15
   facts about, 14–15
   job description, 10–13
   profile of a, 15–16
community college, 8, 25, 35, 67, 129
community garden
   facts about, 91–92
   goals of, 88–89

D

dude ranch, 31, 32–34, 36
   history of, 35

E

ecotourism planner, 40–51
   education/training needed,
      44–45
   job description, 41–43
   profile of a, 45–46

F

fisher, commercial, 20–30
   education/training needed,
      24–26
   facts about, 25
   job description, 21–23
   outlook for, 26–27
   pros/cons of being, 20, 21

G

gardener, urban, 84–95
   education/training needed, 87,
      89–90
   job description, 85–87
groundskeeper, 52–62
   education/training needed, 56–58
   job description, 53–55, 57
   outlook for, 58

H

hotshots, 118, 119

I

internships, 66, 68, 76, 98–99, 119

N

National Park Service, 8, 74, 75–76,
   77, 78, 79, 119–121, 123

P

park ranger, 74–83, 121
   education/training needed, 76–78
   job description, 75–76
   outlook for, 78–80
photographer, nature, 127–137
   code of ethics, 130–131
   education/training needed, 132
   job description, 128–130
   outlook for, 132–133
   profile of a, 133–134

R

ranch hand/wrangler, 31–39
   education/training needed,
      34–36
   job description, 32–34
   outlook for, 36
river guide, 106–116
   job description, 107
   outlook for, 112
   profile of a, 113
   safety code of, 111–112
   training needed, 107–110

S

smoke jumpers, 118, 120–121

T

teacher/naturalist, 63–73
  education/training needed,
    66–68
  job description, 64–66
  profile of a, 68–69
technical/vocational school, 8,
  25–26, 58

W

whales, facts about, 102

whale watcher, 96–105
  education/training needed,
    98–99
  job description, 97–98
  outlook for, 101
whale watching, history of, 100
wildland fire manager,
    117–126
  education/training needed,
    119–121
  job description, 118–119
  outlook for, 122

About the Author

Katie Haegele is a writer who lives in Philadelphia.

Photo Credits

Cover © Francois D'elbee/The Image Bank; pp. 9, 10 © Larry Kolvoord/ The Image Works; p. 12 © Jacksonville Journal Courier; pp. 20, 24 © Terje Rakke/The Image Bank; p. 23 © Josh Reynolds/The Image Works; pp. 31, 33 © David Hamilton/The Image Bank; p. 34 © Tenton Valley Ranch Camp via the Jackson Hole News, File/AP Wide World Photos; pp. 40, 42, 63, 65 © Michael Doolittle/Peter Arnold, Inc.; p. 44 © Dave Bartruff/Index Stock Imagery, Inc.; pp. 52, 54 © Topham/The Image Works; p. 56 © Jack Fields/Corbis; p. 67 © Syracuse Newspapers/The Image Works; pp. 74, 77 © Victoria Arocho/AP Wide World Photos; p. 79 © Tony Gutierrez/AP Wide World Photos; pp. 84, 86 © Joel W. Rogers/Corbis; p. 88 © Bob Daemmrich/The Image Works; pp. 96, 98 © Peter Pereira/AP Wide World Photos; p. 99 © Stephen Frink/Index Stock Imagery, Inc.; p. 102 © Maritime Safety Agency/AP Wide World Photos; pp. 106, 108 © Karl Weatherly/PhotoDisc; p. 110 © Martin Ruetschi/AP Wide World Photos; pp. 117, 120 © Mike McMillan; p. 118 © James L. Amos/Corbis; pp. 127, 129 © Lynn Eodice/Index Stock Imagery; p. 134 © Digital Stock.

Design and Layout

Evelyn Horovicz